TAX FREE AT LAST

A call to the American voters to tell Congress to simplify the tax law, give TAX FREEDOM TO MILLIONS, and then to get their hands around the big fiscal issues. NOW!

John Crone

TAX FREE AT LAST

A call to the American voters to tell Congress to simplify the tax law, give TAX FREEDOM TO MILLIONS, and then to get their hands around the big fiscal issues. NOW!

John Crone

This book is dedicated to the taxpayers of America, who faithfully pay their taxes and file their returns, without question or protest. This book represents their unstated concern: is there a better way?

Table of Contents

Preface

First of all, this book is about taxes. But it is not a book like most every other book about taxes that you have ever read. This is not a book about how to save taxes. Multiple books have been written on how to save taxes about almost every section of the tax law.

Ingenious ideas have been devised and constructed, all to take into account the specifics of a section of the law, and then develop a way around the results that were expected by the people who wrote the law. In fact, a major industry has developed right alongside the growth of the income tax system.

It's kind of an if "you do this" I can work around it type of relationship.

So, in the end, all of this law passing and law avoiding makes for an interesting business, but what does it produce in terms of real productivity for the country?

We all know that reading a book about income tax law can be a very tough assignment and also not that rewarding in terms of the enlightenment of the human soul.

Knowing that, I did not write a book to add to that stack of knowledge about taxes, how to create them and then how to avoid them.

This book is about how to change the tax law so that those citizens at the lower end of the income scale have a better life and more income, not less, as a result of a changed income tax law.

The title of the book is directed at those people who have the least income but are still entangled in the complicated web of income tax compliance. If the recommendations of this book were implemented, taxpayers with less than $100,000 of adjusted gross income would be tax free, no income tax at all.

It's true that in 2020, the top one percent of taxpayers paid 42.3 percent of all income taxes. But that exclusive group also was privileged to earn an average income of almost $550,000 in 2020.

This book is about income equity and taking the yoke off of those with lower income levels. TAX FREE AT LAST!

This book is about how to change the tax law. I want the Congress to finally take a major look at where this train wreck is going and how we can get it under control. The train wreck that I am talking about is the mass of tax laws that have been added and added to the original income tax law created in 1913, over 100 years ago. There are now 2448 pages of tax law, compared to the 14 pages that started this whole program.

Each addition was patched onto the accumulated other changes over the years. Some made sense, but a lot of that really created a patchwork income tax law. A whole bunch of additions were not even related to income taxes as much as they were favorite policies implemented by inclusion in the income tax law.

Such a process would probably work, if someone were writing a letter or an email, and then said, "I think I will slip a new paragraph in the middle here and add another thought." It doesn't work that well, if Congress slips in an addition to the accumulated pages of tax law, and they do it that quite often. The 2017 Tax Cut and Jobs Act added 182 pages of new tax law, as an example. And it is never one or two new thoughts. It is much more complicated than that, laying in new layers of things for the taxpayers to understand.

My first boss, when I came out of the University of Illinois as a Certified Public Accountant and went to work for one of the largest accounting firms in the world, early on gave me a very prescient piece of information. I was researching the tax outcome of a client's business transaction. I didn't like what I had discovered. I said to Paul, this is not fair. He then said "John, never assume that the income tax law is fair." I have personally learned many times over the years that this is very true.

So, this book is not about how to save taxes. It goes deeper than that. This book is about asking our Congress to put some order and common sense in the tax law. Make the law much simpler and understandable.

This book is about asking the individual congress persons to finally take their hands and put them around the gargantuan volume of tax laws and rules. Use their common sense to simplify the law, to make it fairer than it is now, and to use it to collect the revenues needed to meet the government's biggest financial goals.

It could be the last chance to fix this tax system and to get the nation's finances in order. That last point is so very important to all taxpayers. The cover of the book is a depiction of the great Roman Empire's capital in flames. Avoiding that kind of catastrophe is critically important for all taxpayers

The momentum of what is happening in the tax law is tremendous, and it's pointed in the wrong direction.

Right now, Congress has their eye on tweaking the 2017 Tax Cuts and Jobs Act. Some of its provisions were written into the 2017 law to expire in the next two years. Lower tax rates and more tax credits, etc. were put into the law, but they were also written to last for only a few years. If nothing is done, those nice tax cuts will expire by the end of 2025.

So, Congress is saying let's tweak it and then put it back on the bookshelf of tax laws and rules. We can add a few more new pieces, but generally let's fix it for now and push the day of reckoning out a few more years. That's the way things are usually done.

This book advocates a big screeching halt to what we are doing. This is the time to step way back and look at this monster that has grown and grown, without anyone looking at the whole picture.

To say the tax law is complicated is the understatement of the century, literally. It is extremely complicated. It is complicated in following the law, as taxpayers are expected to do. It's complicated in terms of the Congress understanding what they have created. It's complicated when businesses and individuals plan their future decisions. It's complicated when the IRS enforces the tax law. Everything about the U.S. income tax law is complicated.

Let's use this as a stopping point when we address the 2017 tax law expirations, and let's put our hands around it and fix the tax law.

The book lays out many changes that can be made. The book is written to literally pull pages out of the law and burn them.

This is also a time to challenge my first boss, Paul, and say now the tax law is fairer. Make it fair in terms of the distribution of the tax burden and in terms of consistency of who gets taxed.

Lastly, this will be a great time for the Congress to really look at the upward trajectory now in progress of the Federal debt, and the solvency of the Social Security and Medicare systems. There are a lot of things that need to be taken hold of and fixed.

The cover page of this book is intended to be a call for action. The people that need to take action are the people in Congress. The people who can cause those Congress persons to wake up and do something are the voters, the taxpayers. With the implementation of the recommendations in this book, those taxpayers who are in the lower 95% on the income scale will receive a double benefit: Tax Freedom and a stable economy. The upper 1% will receive a stable economy and a country that will be the strongest in the world financially. This is truly a Win-Win opportunity.

Why does the cover depict the scene of Rome burning? It's fairly obvious. Read the book. There are too many major things that are not under control regarding the nation's finances. You can only allow this situation to exist for so long without fixing it. At some point, it becomes unfixable.

Let's give the Congress some major messages. **Get us out of this box. Fix our taxes!**

Introduction

Every author strives to write a great book, a book that holds the reader's attention from start to finish, a book that breaks through with the new ideas that solve major problems, in short, a book that is considered to be a "page turner."

I hope this book is one of those books that opens eyes, provides new understanding, and suggests there actually are good answers to questions   previously thought unsolvable. I hope this book is a "page turner."

I also hope this book is the inspiration to cause its readers to be "page burners."

This book advocates a complete rewrite of the 2448 pages of the Federal income tax code. It will make the case that it is time to reverse 110 years of adding patches here, and new ideas there, with favored citizens changes, social issues, along with popularity efforts all written into the income tax law that started with a law that consumed only 14 pages in 1913.

Here's a review about the environment at the time from Teach Democracy.Org: "Rep. Cordell Hull introduced the first income tax law under the newly adopted Sixteenth Amendment. He proposed a graduated tax starting with a 1-percent rate for incomes between $4,000 and $20,000 increasing to a top rate of 3 percent for those earning $50,000 or more. The House Ways and Means committee called upon citizens to cheerfully support and sustain this, the fairest and cheapest of all taxes.

"The first tax collection day under the new law took place on March 1, 1914. Since the average worker earned only about $800 a year, few people actually had to pay any federal income tax. Less than 4 percent of American families made an annual income of $3,000 or more. Deductions and exemptions further shrank the pool of taxpayers. Nevertheless, the federal government collected $71 million that first year. Millionaire John D. Rockefeller alone paid an estimated $2 million.

"All in all, most Americans thought the new tax was a great idea. One taxpayer wrote to the Bureau of Internal Revenue, "I have purposely left out some deductions I could claim, in order to have the privilege and the pleasure of paying at least a small income tax." (7)

Today, we have a monstrosity of tax laws, regulations, rules, court cases, etc. They represent what is now the 2024 Federal income tax law. Some of the material in this book is provided to give the reader an understanding of the complexity of the tax law. Seeing the pieces that keep piling up, we can see how we got here, and we can see better ways to maintain our income tax system. You will see, as you read this book, that the book says start over. Clear out all of the complications and go back to an understandable set of laws that tax income, in a fair and comprehensible way.

At the end of the book are two free tickets to attend an income tax law page burning party to be held in Washington, D. C. in front of the IRS building at some date in the future. This will happen if the Congress and President pass and sign a new tax law titled "Keep Taxes Simple Stupid (KTSS)" (or some other name, not as clear, perhaps) at some future date. Hope you can make it.

Here is where it all started.

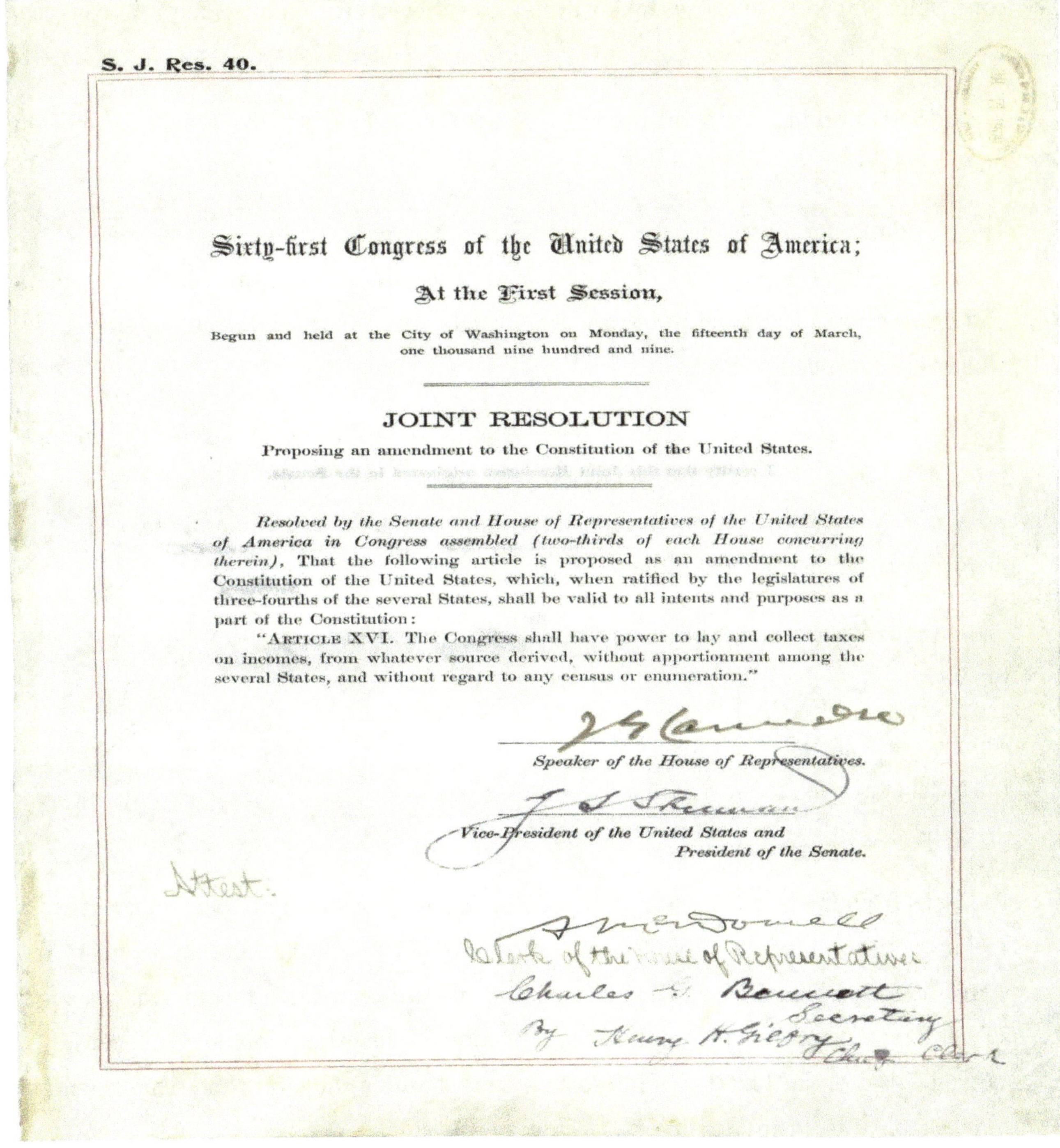

S. J. Res. 40.

Sixty-first Congress of the United States of America;

At the First Session,

Begun and held at the City of Washington on Monday, the fifteenth day of March, one thousand nine hundred and nine.

JOINT RESOLUTION

Proposing an amendment to the Constitution of the United States.

Resolved by the Senate and House of Representatives of the United States of America in Congress assembled (two-thirds of each House concurring therein), That the following article is proposed as an amendment to the Constitution of the United States, which, when ratified by the legislatures of three-fourths of the several States, shall be valid to all intents and purposes as a part of the Constitution:

"ARTICLE XVI. The Congress shall have power to lay and collect taxes on incomes, from whatever source derived, without apportionment among the several States, and without regard to any census or enumeration."

Speaker of the House of Representatives.

Vice-President of the United States and
President of the Senate.

Attest:

From this two paragraph Congressional Joint Resolution, dated March 15, 1909, the seeds were planted for our 2488-page Internal Revenue Code. To paraphrase Winston Churchill: Never in the history of humankind have so many pages of complicated, confusing, and cross-purposes taxing systems ever been created by so few innocent words.

We started out filing very short tax returns in 1913. A copy of the three-page form begins on the next page.

The calculation of the income tax was very straight forward. Add up the sources of income listed as wages, trade or business income, rental income, interest income, gains and profits from partnerships, income from trusts, income derived from any source whatever, not specified above.

Subtract interest expense paid on all debts, state and local taxes, losses incurred from a trade or business, losses from accounts receivable that become worthless, and an amount representing a reasonable allowance for the exhaustion, wear and tear of property used in a trade or business (depreciation),

From that amount an exemption of $3,000 for each taxpayer or $4,000 for a married taxpayer was deducted.

The tax was calculated at rates of 1, 2, 3, 4, 5, and 6% on each tax bracket, with the top 6% bracket applied to income that exceeds $500,000, John D. Rockefeller and maybe a few others.

Proceeds from life insurance were not taxable. Interest on state and local obligations and upon the obligations of the United States were not taxable. Taxing the interest on state and local obligations was considered unconstitutional at the time but that was subsequently determined to not be unconstitutional. The exemption has still been carried forward. The taxation of interest on United States obligations has changed and is now taxable. Life insurance proceeds remain untaxable.

Interesting in this original law, the salary income of the President, and the compensation of judges and all officers and employees of a state or political subdivision were not taxable. Enough said about whether officials of the government receive any special benefits then or now.

With a few exceptions and updates for the current facts, this formula for an income tax law is very close to the sum and substance of the tax reform espoused in the rest of this book.

Maybe we won't get back to the original 14 pages but we will sure carve out a big stack of the current 2,448 pages of the current "income tax" law.

Read on. It can be done. We can get back to an income tax law that taxes income and does not add provisions for various non-income tax policies, preferences, trends, and programs thought to be wonderful ideas, even if they complicate and obliterate the basic formula of paying a tax on income.

Form 1040.

INCOME TAX.

List. No. ....

File No. ....

.... *District of* ....

Assessment List ....

Date received ....

THE PENALTY
FOR FAILURE TO HAVE THIS RETURN IN
THE HANDS OF THE COLLECTOR OF
INTERNAL REVENUE ON OR BEFORE
MARCH 1 IS $20 TO $1,000.
(SEE INSTRUCTIONS ON PAGE 4.)

Page .... *Line* ....

UNITED STATES INTERNAL REVENUE.

RETURN OF ANNUAL NET INCOME OF INDIVIDUALS.

(As provided by Act of Congress, approved October 3, 1913.)

RETURN OF NET INCOME RECEIVED OR ACCRUED DURING THE YEAR ENDED DECEMBER 31, 191 ....

(FOR THE YEAR 1913, FROM MARCH 1, TO DECEMBER 31.)

Filed by (or for) .... *of* ....
(Full name of individual.)   (Street and No.)

in the City, Town, or Post Office of .... *State of* ....
(Fill in pages 2 and 3 before making entries below.)

1. GROSS INCOME (see page 2, line 12)	$
2. GENERAL DEDUCTIONS (see page 3, line 7)	$
3. NET INCOME	$

Deductions and exemptions allowed in computing income subject to the normal tax of 1 per cent.

4. Dividends and net earnings received or accrued, of corporations, etc., subject to like tax. (See page 2, line 11)	$
5. Amount of income on which the normal tax has been deducted and withheld at the source. (See page 2, line 9, column A)	
6. Specific exemption of $3,000 or $4,000, as the case may be. (See Instructions 3 and 19)	
Total deductions and exemptions. (Items 4, 5, and 6)	$
7. TAXABLE INCOME on which the normal tax of 1 per cent is to be calculated. (See Instruction 3)	$

8. When the net income shown above on line 3 exceeds $20,000, the additional tax thereon must be calculated as per schedule below:

	INCOME.	TAX.
1 per cent on amount over $20,000 and not exceeding $50,000	$	$
2 " " 50,000 " " 75,000		
3 " " 75,000 " " 100,000		
4 " " 100,000 " " 250,000		
5 " " 250,000 " " 500,000		
6 " " 500,000		
Total additional or super tax		$
Total normal tax (1 per cent of amount entered on line 7)		$
Total tax liability		$

GROSS INCOME.

This statement must show in the proper spaces the entire amount of gains, profits, and income received by or accrued to the individual from all sources during the year specified on page 1.

DESCRIPTION OF INCOME.	A. Amount of income on which tax has been deducted and withheld at the source.				B. Amount of income on which tax has NOT been deducted and withheld at the source.			
1. Total amount derived from salaries, wages, or compensation for personal service of whatever kind and in whatever form paid	$				$			
2. Total amount derived from professions, vocations, businesses, trade, commerce, or sales or dealings in property, whether real or personal, growing out of the ownership or use of interest in real or personal property, including bonds, stocks, etc.								
3. Total amount derived from rents and from interest on notes, mortgages, and securities (other than reported on lines 5 and 6)								
4. Total amount of gains and profits derived from partnership business, whether the same be divided and distributed or not								
5. Total amount of fixed and determinable annual gains, profits, and income derived from interest upon bonds and mortgages or deeds of trust, or other similar obligations of corporations, joint-stock companies or associations, and insurance companies, whether payable annually or at shorter or longer periods								
6. Total amount of income derived from coupons, checks, or bills of exchange for or in payment of interest upon bonds issued in *foreign countries* and upon *foreign mortgages* or like obligations (not payable in the United States), and also from coupons, checks, or bills of exchange for or in payment of any dividends upon the stock or interest upon the obligations of foreign corporations, associations, and insurance companies engaged in business in foreign countries								
7. Total amount of income received from fiduciaries								
8. Total amount of income derived from any source whatever, not specified or entered elsewhere on this page								
9. TOTALS								

NOTES.—Enter total of Column A on line 5 of first page.

10. AGGREGATE TOTALS OF COLUMNS A AND B	$			
11. Total amount of income derived from dividends on the stock or from the net earnings of corporations, joint-stock companies, associations, or insurance companies subject to like tax (To be entered on line 4 of first page.)	$			
12. TOTAL **"Gross Income"** (to be entered on line 1 of first page)	$			

GENERAL DEDUCTIONS.

1. The amount of necessary expenses actually paid in carrying on business, but not including business expenses of partnerships, and not including personal, living, or family expenses .	$			
2. All interest paid within the year on personal indebtedness of taxpayer				
3. All national, State, county, school, and municipal taxes paid within the year (not including those assessed against local benefits)				
4. Losses actually sustained during the year incurred in trade or arising from fires, storms, or shipwreck, and not compensated for by insurance or otherwise				
5. Debts due which have been actually ascertained to be worthless and which have been charged off within the year				
6. Amount representing a reasonable allowance for the exhaustion, wear, and tear of property arising out of its use or employment in the business, not to exceed, in the case of mines, 5 per cent of the gross value at the mine of the output for the year for which the computation is made, but no deduction shall be made for any amount of expense of restoring property or making good the exhaustion thereof, for which an allowance is or has been made . . .				
7. Total "General Deductions" (to be entered on line 2 of first page)				

AFFIDAVIT TO BE EXECUTED BY INDIVIDUAL MAKING HIS OWN RETURN.

I solemnly swear (or affirm) that the foregoing return, to the best of my knowledge and belief, contains a true and complete statement of all gains, profits, and income received by or accrued to me during the year for which the return is made, and that I am entitled to all the deductions and exemptions entered or claimed therein, under the Federal Income-tax Law of October 3, 1913.

Sworn to and subscribed before me this ....

day of .... , 191

....
(Signature of individual.)

SEAL OF
OFFICER
TAKING
AFFIDAVIT.

....

....
(Official capacity.)

AFFIDAVIT TO BE EXECUTED BY DULY AUTHORIZED AGENT MAKING RETURN FOR INDIVIDUAL.

I solemnly swear (or affirm) that I have sufficient knowledge of the affairs and property of .... to enable me to make a full and complete return thereof, and that the foregoing return, to the best of my knowledge and belief, contains a true and complete statement of all gains, profits, and income received by or accrued to said individual during the year for which the return is made, and that the said individual is entitled, under the Federal Income-tax Law of October 3, 1913, to all the deductions and exemptions entered or claimed therein.

Sworn to and subscribed before me this ....

day of .... , 191

....
(Signature of agent.)

SEAL OF
OFFICER
TAKING
AFFIDAVIT.

....

....
(Official capacity.)

ADDRESS
IN FULL

....

....

[SEE INSTRUCTIONS ON BACK OF THIS PAGE.]

There will be a thousand reasons why the ideas in this book won't work. They will be put forth by the elite, the well connected, the politicians, Wall Street, the lobbyists in Washington. Just look at the composition of the doubters. This group's short name is THE SWAMP.

There are ten thousand reasons why these ideas will work. Try income equity, uplift for the poorest Americans, transparency, simplification, understanding, truth in governing, truthfulness, elimination of layers of bureaucracy, and preserving the solvency of the government. That's a few and they all shine a light on the bottom feeders in THE SWAMP.

We want our great country back and we don't want to be lied to anymore. Example: don't create "The Inflation Reduction Act" and design it in a way that throws fuel on the flames of inflation. Inflation has ravaged all Americans, and it hits the hardest at the Americans at the lowest end of the income scale.

The growth of the size of the tax code and regulations has been outrageous. The increase in IRS agents is oppressive. The cost of compliance is a drag on our nation's productivity.

So, if you want to apply for your social security number, you have to fill out a two-page form. To get a driver's license, you pass a written and driving test, and you get the license. To become a U. S. Citizen, you fill out a 14-page form and pass a written test. To become an attorney or a CPA, you study for several months, take a multi-day test, and you get your accreditation.

To prepare your own tax return, you spend several hours or days each year gathering your data. You consult the instructions for preparing your return. Publication 17 titled "Your Income Tax" alone goes 140 pages. Depending on the components of your return, you may have to understand many more pages of law, regulation, and instructions.

According to Pew Research Center, "the rules governing what constitutes business or individual income, and how it should be taxed, are only part of what makes the U. S. tax code as complex as it is. One rough measure of that complexity: The printed version of the 2021 edition of the Internal Revenue Code runs a total of 4,074 pages. More than half of those pages (2,448) are devoted to the income tax alone." (1)

So only 2,448 pages of tax code, and you or your tax return preparer should be able to take a good try at preparing your tax return; not so fast. Don't forget the thousands of pages of IRS issued rules and regulations, and the thousands of court cases that help define a proper execution of your tax return.

Looking strictly at the Internal Revenue Code, it has grown from two paragraphs in 1909, to the 14 pages in the first tax law in 1914 passed after ratification of the 16th amendment to the Constitution to the 2,448 pages noted above. I doubt if those poor, innocent lawmakers realized then what a monster they were giving birth to and foisting on the American public.

In 1921, seven years into the evolution of the income tax law, a revision to the income tax code was passed and it totaled 108 pages. The tax law book was growing. E. E. Rossmoor, former Chief of the IRS Special Audit Section, wrote a book to explain the new law.

In the preface to his book, explaining the revised tax law in his book's 410 pages, he said "The present Congress has achieved the seemingly impossible task of passing an income tax law even more complicated than its already far too complicated predecessor. And so, the taxpayer finds himself confronted with the task of meeting the requirements of a statute that even the expert will have difficulty in unravelling." (2)

Little did even Mr. Rossmoor know then, as he saw the complications of one of the first attempts to update the new income law, that this early step was leading down a long road to tax law insanity. Yet here we are, staring down a pile of thousands of pages of income tax law chapters and verses. Maybe artificial intelligence is arriving just in time. Even the big computer is no match for our politicians' talent to complicate our lives.

Just over 100 years later, William McBride, Vice president of Federal Tax Policy at the Tax Foundation, concluded his testimony to the U. S. Senate Committee on Finance with this comment: "We, as a country have built a federal tax system that is inherently complex, costly, and controversial, one that is centered on taxing both individual and business income at progressive tax rates and littered with various preferences. To the extent it is comprehensible at all, **taxpayers do not perceive it as fair**. The IRS has challenges administering such a complicated tax system, but boosting the IRS budget will not fix the underlying problem that causes taxpayers to call (into) the IRS millions of time per year asking for help filing tax forms that take them more than 6.5 billion hours to complete." (3)

Here is the Big Reveal: the income tax law is not an income tax law. It is a grab bag of laws as misnamed as the Inflation Reduction Law, mentioned above. What does buying an electric vehicle and getting a gift from the government have to do with income taxes? Why does encouraging the production of oil give the oil well owner a gift of reduced income taxes via the depletion allowance? Bigger question yet, did anyone ever notice these two components in the income tax law work in direct conflict with each other?

The Wall Street Journal said it well when they noted "there are many reasons for (the overwhelming income tax complexity). The tax code reflects the intricacies of modern financial and social life, and it's also a mishmash of competing policy interests that shift over time and often interact in unexpected ways." (4)

The Journal points to the simple factor of human nature. In the large U. S. economy, there are always conflicting interests. One part of the economy might see a law as a well-deserved tax incentive and someone else might decry that same law as a wasteful tax break.

These opposing factions feed the industry of lobbyists fighting for the important issues of their clients. For every side, there are often hundreds of different lobbyists and eventually the Congress meets some or all of one faction's demands and writes new law favoring the winning faction. Then, when a taxpayer takes advantage of a tax break written into the law, what happens? Oftentimes, the media, or the opposing faction highlights the "terrible taxpayer" for taking advantage of tax law that is clearly allowed. So, it's a never-ending cycle, the lawmakers rise and pass a new law, adding to the web of tax laws already in existence.

The Alternative Minimum Tax is a prime example. It basically says once you have determined your taxable income and the tax thereon, then you need to recalculate your alternative minimum taxable income, which basically takes back several tax breaks allowed in the calculation of "regular" taxable income.

Now the lawmakers have come up with a way to take back what was given and to ensnare those taxpayers that calculated their taxes, according to the tax law. Now they realized they could rerun them through a different calculation. The lawmakers saw that as another way to confuse and raise income.

In 2022, Congress created the "Adjusted Financial Statement Income" calculation. This makes sure the tax paid by a corporation sweeps in any difference between income reported to shareholders, and income reported to the IRS. Once again, why create tax laws and then effectively reverse them with a second, third recalculation? It's literally a perverse system.

To understand the creation of our income tax law, all you have to do is follow the money.

The factions and their lobbyists get to the Congress members and win their case on a given day. How many hours and dollars are spent every year in this crazy endeavor? You don't want to know. Suffice to say, the cost is enormous and it comes out of the pockets of the American public, one way or another. For that, we get a convoluted tax system beyond the grasp of human or artificial intelligence. One recent estimate of the annual cost of lobbying was over $4.2 Billion. (4) Add to that 165 million taxpayer hours per year to prepare their returns and some unknown billions of dollars paid to professional tax return preparers and tax audit advisers. Do we really need this much complication? I don't think so.

1. What is an Income Tax Law?

An income tax law is a law that collects income taxes from citizens based on the amount of income they receive. In simple terms if someone earns taxable income of $100,000, and the income tax law collects 20% of the income, the law provides for the taxpayer to pay $20,000.

That is simple enough. That is what we need to get back to. We need to slice and whack and squeeze every non income tax law out of our income tax laws. Example: if our lawmakers think the federal government should have some responsibility for encouraging its citizens to buy electric vehicles, pass a law to accomplish that. But keep that law out of the income tax law. Instead, pass a law called the Electric Vehicle Buying Incentive Law. This is totally separate from income taxes. Maybe the car dealer cuts the price $7500 per vehicle and then submits a monthly report to the Transportation Department for a check of $7500 for every electric vehicle sold. That would take many pages out of the Income Tax Law, simplifying the preparation of the return of a taxpayer who did or didn't buy an electric vehicle.

It would also clarify what is the cost of subsidizing EV production. It would also provide transparency to all. The government wants to pay you $7500 to buy an electric vehicle. You get it at the dealer, not the IRS.

Now, maybe in some other area, some part of the American public may not like a benefit that is being provided in the income tax law. It may be hard to find it if it is being done in a way that the benefit is buried within the income tax law.

There are a host of just such benefits purposely crafted and buried in the income tax law. Many are good and appropriate (depending on your point of view), but they are also sensitive issues (depending on your point of view).

If these non-income law benefits are buried in the income tax law, one obvious result is no one knows how much is being spent on the benefit or who is getting the reward of that non income tax law benefit. These benefits or costs are buried in the net IRS collections.

Some might say that is an ingenious way to get things done in Washington. Hide the ball. Put this and that on the Christmas tree. One more ornament on a very big tree. It's too complicated. We all work on or pay to have others prepare our tax returns. We don't move beyond our own tax refund or payment and think about what has been done to us.

The federal budget states we have budgeted to spend $6.1 Trillion in fiscal 2023. That does not include the Billions of dollars that the government collects from taxpayers and conveniently returns in the form of tax credits and tax deductions. That is a big cost that never gets reported.

The government reports it is spending $6.1 Trillion or 23% of the country's total production as defined by the 2023 estimate of GNP. No, that is just not true. It is also collecting an additional Billions of dollars and disbursing those collections through the process of the "income tax" law.

2. The Stage is Already Set for Major Changes in Our Income Tax Law.

That is because many provisions of the 2017 Tax Cuts and Jobs Act of 2017 (TCJA) are set to expire in 2025. Congress will need to extend or sunset these provisions.

Chickens do come home to roost. That will not come as a big surprise to those who govern us in Washington. Congress often justifies new tax laws by running them through the House Congressional Budget Office (CBO). The goal is to have the new legislation be revenue neutral or even, in some instances, to project a reduction in the federal deficit.

According to the CBO's website, "the CBO is required to produce a cost estimate for nearly every bill approved by a full committee of the House of Representative and the Senate. Cost estimates are advisory only. They can, but need not be, used to enforce budgetary rules or targets."

There is a saying that "figures don't lie but liars do figure." The quote is often attributed to Mark Twain, in 1910, four years before the passage of the first income tax law. But that quote actually goes back to 1889, according to research done by Quote Investigator. (6).

"Carroll D. Wright was a prominent statistician employed by the U. S. Government, and he provided us with the expression in 1889 while addressing the Convention of Commissioners of Bureaus of Statistics of Labor. In that testimony, he stated "the old saying is that figures will not lie, but a new saying is liars will figure. It is our duty, as practical statisticians, to prevent the liar from figuring; in other words, to prevent him from perverting the truth, in the interest of some theory he wishes to establish."

Wright was right in defining the duty of that bureau, but he was seriously underestimating the ability of the liars, in future years, to come up with ways to get the right results by doing some creative accounting; That is, lying with a straight face and pure demeanor.

That gets us back to the TCJA.

Many of the 2017 tax law provisions expire in 2025 setting up a need to address the expirations and relook at the income tax law. The TCJA was passed in the first year of President Trump's term of office. It occurred when the Republicans had a majority in the Senate and the House of Representatives.

The TCJA brought tax relief to individuals and businesses, but the act also left a ticking time bomb in the middle of the income tax law. That time bomb was one of the many provisions in the law that were written to expire in 2025.

Why change the tax law in 2017 only to eliminate the changes in 2025? That's kind of how Washington works. One phrase is 'kicking the can down the road." The reason for the time bomb in the new tax law is that Congress wanted the CBO cost estimate of the tax act to show that it was revenue neutral.

This goal was accomplished not by putting enough provisions in the law to increase federal revenue as an offset to tax cuts. It was accomplished by putting the tax cuts in the law but also providing for them to expire in eight years. The effect of all this manipulation was that the CBO estimate turned out to be revenue neutral. Of course, many of the tax cut provisions have turned out to be popular and desirable.

Do you see that big can that is bouncing down the road aiming right at the current Congress in 2025? Now the new Congress has to deal with the expirations, call them artificial expirations that justified the CBO cost estimate as being revenue neutral.

Was this congressional sleight of hand just a maneuver at the time to pass the 2017 TCJA? Or did it also set in place an opportunity for Congress to be courted by lobbyists who represent those that would be adversely affected by the expiration of the TCJA provisions?

Here's how The Tax Foundation describes the situation: "Congress has less than two years to prevent tax hikes on the vast majority of Americans from taking place. That's because the Tax Cuts and Jobs Act (TCJA) of 2017, a tax reform law that simplified individual income taxes and reduced tax rates across the income spectrum, is set to expire. If Congress does nothing, most Americans will face higher taxes, worse incentives for work and investment, and a more complicated tax system starting in 2026.

"The TCJA reduced average tax rates for taxpayers at all income levels because it lowered marginal tax rates, widened tax brackets, doubled the child tax credit and zeroed out personal and dependent exemptions, nearly doubled the standard deduction, and limited several itemized deductions and the alternative minimum tax, among other changes. Although not every change the TCJA made was a tax cut—for instance, placing a $10,000 cap on itemized deductions for state and local taxes paid increased taxable income for higher-income taxpayers living in high-tax states—the net effect of all changes taken together was to reduce average tax burdens.

"In 2017, the year before the new tax changes took effect, the bottom half of taxpayers paid an <u>average tax rate</u> of 4.0 percent. After the TCJA took effect in 2018, the average tax rate for the bottom half dropped to 3.4 percent. Likewise, the average tax rate paid by the top 1 percent of taxpayers decreased from 26.8 percent in 2017 to 25.4 percent in 2018. Average rates declined across all income groups and have remained below their 2017 levels since. Further, we estimate making the individual provisions of the TCJA permanent would reduce taxes for about 62 percent of filers, leave taxes unchanged for about 29 percent, and increase taxes for just under 9 percent of filers in 2026.

"If Congress does nothing, most Americans will face higher taxes, worse incentives for work and investment, and a more complicated tax system starting in 2026."

This is exactly the wrong direction to take the tax law. We need to simplify, reduce the size of the tax law, and be fair to all taxpayers

So now the process begins. Another last-minute solution no doubt will be agreed to sometime in early 2026, just in time for taxpayers to incorporate all of the patches, changes, and solutions brought to bear, in backroom meetings, bars and restaurants. Lobbyists for all parts of the tax law will court and pressure the legislators.

Maybe we are a little jaded here in our outlook. Certainly, the history of similar situations in the recent years, suggests we will end up with a last-minute fix, 100's of new pages, and all brought to us in the middle of the night, with little chance for review, discussion or understanding. That's now the way things are done in general.

Regarding our most likely addition to the tax law, it will be a poorly designed, hastily constructed bolt on structure added to the Rube Goldberg monstrosity that has been built in a similar manner over the last 110 years of tax law.

"A **Rube Goldberg machine**, named after American cartoonist Rube Goldberg, is a chain reaction–type machine or contraption intentionally designed to perform a simple task in an indirect and (impractically) overly complicated way. Usually, these machines consist of a series of simple unrelated devices; the action of each triggers the initiation of the next, eventually resulting in achieving a stated goal."

That seems to be a very accurate description of our tax law, yet to be modified again by the expiration of the 2017 TCJA.

Appendix A to this book shows the list of the expiring provisions in the Tax Cuts and Jobs Act. The appendix is a Congressional Research Service report prepared for members and committees of Congress.

In the introductory section of the report is a summary of the budgetary cost of the Act as follows:

"At the time of the law's passage, the Joint Committee on Taxation (JCT) estimated that the TCJA would cost $1.5 Trillion between FY2018 and FY2027. 1 The Congressional Budget Office (CBO) and JCT have estimated that extensions of all provisions that are scheduled to either expire or become less generous would cost $3.5 Trillion between FY2023 and FY2033, although most of these effects would begin in FY2026."

They knew then what the cost of the extensions of these tax benefits would cost, but they closed their eyes and assumed the future Congress would not extend the tax benefits. Bad assumption. Now the 2025 Congress has that very job of looking at the expiring benefits and deciding what to do.

Professor Butts and the Self-Operating ladle (C), which throws cracker (D) past toucan (E). Toucan jumps after cracker and Napkin (1931). Soup spoon (A) is raised to mouth, pulling string (B) and thereby jerking perch (F) tilts, upsetting seeds (G) into pail (H). Extra weight in pail pulls cord (I), which opens and ignites lighter (J), setting off skyrocket (K), which causes sickle (L) to cut string (M), allowing pendulum with attached napkin to swing back and forth, thereby wiping chin.

You can look at the Appendix and see what is at stake. To mention the more significant provisions, here is a shorter list of expiring provisions from the TCJA:

1. The lower tax rates.
2. The higher standard deduction.
3. The elimination of personal exemptions.
4. Higher child tax credits.
5. Changes in deductions for charitable contributions.
6. Limit of $10,000 for state and local tax (SALT) deductions.
7. Reduction of certain limits on mortgage interest deductions.
8. Elimination of a cap on the deduction of itemized deductions.
9. Reduction of the exposure to personal alternative minimum tax.
10. The deduction of the 20% reduction of business pass through income.
11. Elimination of the deduction of excess business losses.
12. Allowance of full expensing and then reduced percentage of property used in a trade or business otherwise deductible as depreciation.
13. Increased exemption for estate and gift taxes.
14. Establishment of Qualified opportunity zones.

Here's the Question: Is this a very rare and unique opportunity to create a simpler, understandable overhaul of the tax code? Or do we keep marching down the path of craziness?

3. A New Path Forward

Here's the Answer: Let's spend the 2024-25 years building a new income tax law.

That's not what the lawmakers are thinking. In an article in the Wall Street Journal on April 12, 2024, Kevin Hardy, who was the chair of the House Ways and Means Committee when the TCJA was written and passed, highlighted the 2024 expirations of several provisions in the law. His suggestions are basically to renew the expirations and fine tune the tax law a little more. Is that hypocritical since he wrote the expirations to begin with to get around guardrails intended to require prudent fiscal spending? Is that conventional thinking, to adjust and tinker? This is the time to fix the whole mess.

In this book, we put the spotlight on some of the most complicated parts of our tax laws. Take a look. Can we change our system? What if we do it and actually do establish a revenue neutral income tax law – not a can to be kicked down the road for a future Congresses to clean up.

Let's do a real redo, that will be reviewed by the Congressional Budget Office and that will be projected to provide adequate revenue to the government, a program for reduction of the national debt, wholesale simplification, and fairness to all participants in the economy.

It's very appropriate to quote Daniel Burnham, a Chicago architect (1864-1912):

"Make no small plans. They have no magic to stir men's blood and probably themselves will not be realized. Make big plans: aim high in hope and work, remembering that a noble, logical diagram once recorded will never die, but long after we are gone will be a living thing, asserting itself with ever-growing insistency. Remember that our sons and grandsons are going to do things that would stagger us. Let your watchword be order and your beacon beauty. **Think Big."**

This can be done by literally starting with a blank sheet of paper. The Congressional Budget Office has files and files about the tax revenues, the tax deductions, the economy, and incomes. Computers have the capacity to game out various scenarios and measure projected results. Artificial intelligence can put forth ideas, history, and projections of the future.

And, here's the Big One, what if we throw out 2488 pages of tax law and put in a lot fewer pages; we can understand what we have, and we can calculate much more accurately the results of the tax system.

Boil it down to much fewer variables, and it really becomes a determination of tax rates for individuals on a progressive scale and for corporations based on their income without special deductions, social goals, multiple accounting methods, and a host of other complicating factors.

If Congress does implement the ideas of a higher standard deduction and return of the personal exemptions, millions of taxpayers will file much simpler short form tax returns. That will reduce the compliance burden for the lower income taxpayers (less than $100,000 of income). There will be major reduction in the work load of the IRS in processing such simple tax returns. In the next section of this book, we will examine many of the complicated parts of the tax law. With our focus on simplification and our tool of being able to calculate the results of our changes, we will take a huge sledgehammer to most of the current complications.

We will not cover all 2488 pages of the law but we will create a process of looking at the big pieces.

In addition, this proposal should be known to the American public during the 2024 presidential and congressional elections. It would be great if both major candidates became leaders of the need for reform. It would be an opportunity for those individuals running for the House and Senate to say, "Yah we can make this happen." Let's all rise to the occasion and let's gain the momentum that is needed to make this happen.

4. Slice, Slice and then Slice Some More

168 million individual tax returns were filed in 2022.

The effective tax rates reported by increments in the adjusted gross income reported on Form 1040, reported by the Pew Research Center, based on all returns, for 2000-2020 are shown below. This was for a group of returns filed for a 20-year period, affected by changes in the tax laws during that time including the TCJA tax law in 2017.

The charts below show what the effective rates were, what the current scheduled tax brackets are, and the charts also show how those rates could be adjusted to provide new rates going into the future:

Adjusted Gross Income Group	Effective tax rate
$5M+	26.13%
$500K-5.M	25.55%
$200K-500K	16.77%
$100K-200K	10.04%
$50K-100K	7.29%
$30K-50K	4.29%
$15K-30K	1.96%
$1-15K	.21%

The above effective rates were the result of including all of the tax brackets up to the highest-income bracket, and also including other provisions including tax credits and tax-exempt income and capital gain rates, etc.

Current Tax Tables

Tax Rate	For Single Filers	For Joint Returns
10%	$0 to $11,600	$0 to $23,200
12%	$11,600 to $47,150	$23,200 to $94,300
22%	$47,150 to $100,525	$94,300 to $201,050
24%	$100,525 to $191,950	$201,050 to $383,900
32%	$191,950 to $243,725	$383,900 to $487,450
35%	$243,725 to $609,350	$487,450 to $731,200
37%	$609,350 or more	$731,200 or more

<u>**For Heads of Households**</u>

$0 to $16,550
$16,550 to $63,100
$63,100 to $100,500

$100,500 to $191,950

$191,950 to $243,700
$243,700 to $609,350
$609,350 or more

One purpose of this book is to simplify the tax rate schedules by having one set of rates for all tax returns, whether single, married, head of household, or surviving spouse.

Every return would carry the same rates as those used on the current single filer tax returns (see discussion later in the book). In addition, all income would be taxed at those rates. Including capital gains, interest income on state and local obligations, and carried interest income.

<u>**New Tax Tables**</u>

Current Tax Rate	**For All Filers**	**New Tax Rates**
NA	-$100,000 to $0	-10%
10%	$0 to $11,600	Same
12%	$11,600 to $47,150	Same
22%	$47,150 to $100,525	Same
24%	$100,525 to $191,950	Same
32%	$191,950 to $243,725	Same
35%	$243,725 to $400,000	38%
35-37%	$400,000 or more	41%

The increase in rates in the two highest brackets is intended to replace the Net Investment Income Tax of 3.8% (see discussion later in the book)'. The $400,000 cut off would comply with President Biden's pledge to not raise taxes below that income level.

Negative taxable income up to $100K will create a tax refund of 10%. This negative rate could be adjusted higher but needs to be coordinated with other assistance programs. This will be a tremendous help to the Americans at the lower end of the income scale.

Lawmakers are continually tinkering with the tax rates in order to stimulate the economy, slow down inflation, more "fairly distribute the tax burden," soak the rich or help those in greater need.

It's great to be able to turn up the temperature or turn it down if you are baking a tuna casserole in the oven. It's terribly disruptive and costly if you are playing with the United States economy.

American taxpayers, like football and basketball players, or like a table for four bridge card players, or like kids in fourth grade, all of them need to know what the rules are. You can't change them from year to year or during the game. That would lead to very bad results.

The same is just as true if not critically true for the income tax system. Individuals and corporations do their planning based on a longer-term horizon than the rapidity of current tax law changes would dictate. It would be tremendously beneficial to have a stable tax rate system, incorporated with a much simpler income tax system.

It's not a nuclear physicist level type of requirement to determine a reasonable set of tax brackets and make that the law of the land. Let those who make the most have the higher tax rates but also continue to provide incentive to all taxpayers to do better on the economic scale.

Also, it's important to assist those with low incomes to be able to raise their economic status and more importantly to enjoy their lives with enough income to meet some more comfortable standard of living. The tax rates need to go easy on those with lesser income. Tax freedom and reduction in tax return compliance will be of great benefit to these less fortunate citizens.

The tax rates need to continue to provide incentive to those with high income to reinvest in the economy. The rates also need to provide low enough rates to help those with less than adequate income. Thus, the tax rate schedule will provide negative tax rates for those showing a negative income after deduction of an $80,000 standard deduction and $5,000 personal exemptions

How much should the tax rates "soak the rich?" William McBride (Vice President of Federal Tax Policy at the Tax Foundation), in his testimony to Congress on November 9, 2023, reported that "by any measure, the tax code is extremely progressive and very redistributive…. The top 5 percent of taxpayers (about 7.9 million filers who earn more than $220,521) paid…62.7% of all income taxes (in 2020)." The top 1 percent's share of income was 42.3 percent of all income taxes. (3)

The testimony of Mr. McBride and his associate, Stephen J. Entin, provided is so informative and so on point regarding the need for tax reform, that it has been included in this book as Appendix B.

The proposed tax rates are suggested to provide more revenue to the government by increasing the effective tax rates for those taxpayers with more than $400,000 of taxable income. The increase is significant but not confiscatory in any stretch of the imagination. Projections should be made by the Congressional Budget Office to see what the net effect of the total reform package will be. That is always the case with any legislation, and if a major reform package is passed, it can be tested and evaluated. That's true whether the package includes changes noted in this book or some other changes.

The goals, besides cleaning up the Rube Goldberg contraption called the current income tax system should be to:

1. Cover the cost of lowering the tax rates for the lower income taxpayers.
2. Provide additional income to be used for such important objectives as;
    a. Lowering the annual budget deficit, and national debt,
    b. Beginning a program to pay down the unfunded obligations of the Social Security and Medicare programs.
3. Protect the tax laws from being subject to constant change.

4. Protect the tax laws from being used as a way to implement political social policies not a part of the income tax law.
5. Create a tax system that will help focus on the financial well-being of the country and reduce laws and policies that are in conflict with that goal.

5. 3.8% Net investment Income Tax

The tax law added the 3.8% net investment income tax in 2013.This tax was added as a revenue offset to the Affordable Care Act. The 3.8% tax is applied to net investment income in excess of a threshold amount of $200,000 for singles or $250,000 for married filing jointly. Investment income includes taxable interest, dividends, capital gains, even taxable gain on the sale of a home.

All of this added another calculation in arriving at the total income tax due for the year. The taxpayer has to go down a separate path and total their net investment income, compare that to the threshold amount, and the difference is taxed at the 3.8% rate.

Although the tax was added to help pay for the Affordable Care Act, the tax collections are added to the general fund revenues and not separately accounted for in an Affordable Care "lock box."

As with all complications to the process of calculating a taxpayer's total tax, this additional calculation should be dropped and the base tax rate should be adjusted to replace the tax revenues from the net investment income tax.

6. Eliminate the differences in tax rates for married, single, head of household

Currently there are different tax rates for whether the taxpayer files as a single person, files jointly with their spouse, two spouses file separately, files as a surviving spouse, or files as a head of household.

Why? When a married couple walks into Best Buy and purchases a wide screen TV, do they pay a different sales tax than the single person or the unmarried couple? Same with property taxes?

The income tax law should tax the income and not the marital status of the taxpayer. This change will cut the number of tax tables in the tax law by 80%. That is simplification and fairness for all.

In addition, the game of determining whether two people should get married will be over. There are actually computer programs that calculate what taxes will result whether two people are filing jointly or as singles.

The marriage vow, with the current income tax law, apparently has to go as follows:

I, _____, take you, _____, to be my wife (or husband), to have and to hold from this day forward, for better, for worse, for richer, for poorer, in sickness and in health, to love and to cherish, till death us do part, according to God's holy law, and this is my solemn vow, **as long as the union does not result in higher income taxes.**

7. Determining who is a taxpayer's dependent should be simplified and taxpayers should get a personal exemption for each dependent.

Dependents should be defined as anyone for whom the taxpayer provides more than half of their support and who are citizens, resident aliens, or a U.S. National. More than one person cannot claim the same dependent.

Personal exemptions were eliminated from 2018-2025 by the TCJA. This is one of the provisions that will return as an expired provision of the act beginning in 2026. This should be allowed to happen. Each personal exemption amounted to $4,150 in 2018.The exemption amount is adjusted each year for inflation.

On the following page is a chart that guides a taxpayer to determine if an individual is dependent and also if the taxpayer could file as a head of household or surviving spouse. The filing status determination would be made unnecessary by the proposed change to have all taxpayers use the same tax table. The question of who a dependent is will also be greatly simplified by the more than half support question discussed above. The following chart goes away. It's a "One for All" plan regarding filing status and a "One for half plus" regarding the determination of dependents and personal exemptions.

The IRS provides charts to help determine if the taxpayer has a qualifying child and if that child can be claimed as a dependent and to find out if your dependent qualifies you to take the child care credit or the credit for other dependents. The charts, which are meant to help the taxpayer, are in themselves, complicated. It really is time to simplify the tax laws.

Chart 1

Federal Income Tax Rules
For Claiming Dependents and
Determining Filing Status

	Requirements	Age	Residency	Support	Gross income of possible dependent	Special Case
Definition of Dependent	Not a dependent of another taxpeyer, not filing a joint return, except to get a refund of estimated tazwa oe withholding, must be a US citizen, US resident alien, US national, or resident of Canada or Mexico, (also an exception for certain adopted children.)					
A. Qualifying Child, or	Must be taxpapyer son, daughter, steppchild, foster child, brother, sister, half brother, half sister, stepbrother, stepsister, or a descendent of any of them.	Under 19 at end of year, under age 24 at end of year if a full-time student and younger than the taxpayer or taxpayer's spouse, , any age if permanently and totally disabled.	Must have lived with the taxpayer more than half the year or half of time the person was alive.	Person must not have provided more than half of their own support for the year. Taxpayer doesn't have to have provided any of the support.		If the poterntial dependent meets the rules to be a qualifying child of more than one person, must be entitled to claim per the tiebraker rules. There is not choice if the qualifying parent has the higher AGI, if no parent is invollved goe to the taxpayer with the highest AGI.
B. A Qualifying Relative	Not a qualifying child of taxpayer or any other taxpayer. Must be related to the taxpayer/spouse as a child, stepchild, foster child, or a descendent of any of them, or borther/sister, stepbrother/sister, half brother/sister, or father, mother, grandparent, o other diredt ancestor, but not foster parent, stefather-mother, so or daughter of a bother/sister or half brother/sister, or brother or sister of the taxpayers/spouse's father or mother, or son in law daughter in law, father in law mother in law, brother or sister in law. Cousin doesn't count. Or counts if person has lived with the taxpayer legally as a member of their household all year.	NA		The taxpayer must provide more than half of the support for the year, compared to all other sources including welfare. Exceptios for multiple support agreements and kinapped children.	Must be less than $4,700	
Head of Household Requirements	Unmarried or considered unmarried on the last day of the tax year. Had a qualifying person live with the taxpayer in the home more than half of the year, except for temporary absences. A qualfying person is child who is single or is married and can be claimed as a dependent, a brother, sister, step brother or sister, father or mother, or ancestor of either, step father or mother, son or daugher of a brother or sister, brother or sister of the father or mother of the taxpayer, or is a parent of the taxpayer, if the taxpayer paid more than half the cost of maintaining that parent's main home for the entire year and is claimed as a dependent on the taxpayer's return.		The taxpayer can't be a nonresident alien for any part of the year.	Paid more than half of the cost of maintaining the home for the year		A marrried considered unmarried taxpayer has fewer options for a qualifying person and they are child, stepchild or foster child who lived with the taxpayer for more than half the year.
Surviving Spouse Requirements	Can claim for two years following death of spouse, if did not remarry in that time period. Taxpayer must have a child or step child that can be claimed as a dependent or could claim as a dependent except the child had gross inome of $4400 or more, the child filed a joint return, or the child could be claimed as a dependent on someone else's return. This child must have lived in taxpayer's home all year except for temporary absensces. Taxpayer must have paid more than half of the cost of keeping up the home for the year.					

Chart 2

Who Qualifies as Your Dependent

Dependents, Qualifying Child for Child Tax Credit, and Credit for Other Dependents

Follow the steps below to find out if a person qualifies as your dependent and to find out if your dependent qualifies you to take the child tax credit or the credit for other dependents. If you have more than four dependents, check the box under *Dependents* on page 1 of Form 1040 or 1040-SR and include a statement showing the information required in columns (1) through (4).

 *The dependents you claim are those you list by name and SSN in the* Dependents *section on Form 1040 or 1040-SR.*

Before you begin. See the definition of *Social security number*, later. If you want to claim the child tax credit or the credit for other dependents, you (and your spouse if filing jointly) must have an SSN or ITIN issued on or before the due date of your 2023 return (including extensions). If an ITIN is applied for on or before the due date of a 2023 return (including extensions) and the IRS issues an ITIN as a result of the application, the IRS will consider the ITIN as issued on or before the due date of the return.

Step 1 Do You Have a Qualifying Child?

A qualifying child is a child who is your...

Son, daughter, stepchild, foster child, brother, sister, stepbrother, stepsister, half brother, half sister, or a descendant of any of them (for example, your grandchild, niece, or nephew)

was ...

Under age 19 at the end of 2023 and younger than you
(or your spouse if filing jointly)

or

Under age 24 at the end of 2023, a student (defined later), and younger than you
(or your spouse if filing jointly)

or

Any age and permanently and totally disabled (defined later)

Who didn't provide over half of their own support for 2023 (see Pub. 501)

Who isn't filing a joint return for 2023
or is filing a joint return for 2023 only to claim a refund of withheld income tax or estimated tax paid (see Pub. 501 for details and examples)

Who lived with you for more than half of 2023. If the child didn't live with you for the required time, see *Exception to time lived with you*, later.

 *If the child meets the conditions to be a qualifying child of any other person (other than your spouse if filing jointly) for 2023, see* Qualifying child of more than one person, *later.*

1. Do you have a child who meets the conditions to be your qualifying child?

    ☐ **Yes.** Go to Step 2.   ☐ **No.** Go to Step 4.

Chart 3

Step 2 **Is Your Qualifying Child Your Dependent?**

1. Was the child a U.S. citizen, U.S. national, U.S. resident alien, or a resident of Canada or Mexico? (See Pub. 519 for the definition of a U.S. national or U.S. resident alien. If the child was adopted, see *Exception to citizen test*, later.)

☐ **Yes.** Continue ↓

☐ **No.** (STOP) You can't claim this child as a dependent.

2. Was the child married?

☐ **Yes.** See *Married person*, later.

☐ **No.** Continue ↓

3. Are you filing a joint return for 2023?

☐ **Yes.** You can claim this child as a dependent. Complete columns (1) through (3) of the *Dependents* section on page 1 of Form 1040 or 1040-SR for this child. Then, go to Step 3.

☐ **No.** Continue ↓

4. Could you be claimed as a dependent on someone else's 2023 tax return? (If the person who could claim you on their 2023 tax return is not required to file, and isn't filing a 2023 tax return or is filing a 2023 return only to claim a refund of withheld income tax or estimated tax paid, check "No.") See Steps 1, 2, and 4.

☐ **Yes.** (STOP) You can't claim any dependents. Complete the rest of Form 1040 or 1040-SR and any applicable schedules.

☐ **No.** You can claim this child as a dependent. Complete columns (1) through (3) of the *Dependents* section on page 1 of Form 1040 or 1040-SR for this child. Then, go to Step 3.

Step 3 **Does Your Qualifying Child Qualify You for the Child Tax Credit or Credit for Other Dependents?**

1. Did the child have an SSN, ITIN, or adoption taxpayer identification number (ATIN) issued on or before the due date of your return (including extensions)? (Answer "Yes" if you are applying for an ITIN or ATIN for the child on or before the due date of your return (including extensions).)

☐ **Yes.** Continue ↓

☐ **No.** (STOP) You can't claim the child tax credit or the credit for other dependents for this child.

2. Was the child a U.S. citizen, U.S. national, or U.S. resident alien? (See Pub. 519 for the definition of a U.S. national or U.S. resident alien. If the child was adopted, see *Exception to citizen test*, later.)

☐ **Yes.** Continue ↓

☐ **No.** (STOP) You can't claim the child tax credit or the credit for other dependents for this child.

3. Was the child under age 17 at the end of 2023?

☐ **Yes.** Continue ↓

☐ **No.** You can claim the credit for other dependents for this child. Check the "Credit for other dependents" box in column (4) of the *Dependents* section on page 1 of Form 1040 or 1040-SR for this person.

4. Did this child have an SSN valid for employment issued before the due date of your 2023 return (including extensions)? (See *Social Security Number*, later.)

☐ **Yes.** You can claim the child tax credit for this person. Check the "Child tax credit" box in column (4) of the *Dependents* section on page 1 of Form 1040 or 1040-SR for this person.

☐ **No.** (STOP) You can claim the credit for other dependents for this child. Check the "Credit for other dependents" box in column (4) of the *Dependents* section on page 1 of Form 1040 or 1040-SR for this person.

Chart 4

Step 4 Is Your Qualifying Relative Your Dependent?

A qualifying relative is a person who is your...

Son, daughter, stepchild, foster child, or a descendant of any of them (for example, your grandchild)

or

Brother, sister, half brother, half sister, or a son or daughter of any of them (for example, your niece or nephew)

or

Father, mother, or an ancestor or sibling of either of them (for example, your grandmother, grandfather, aunt, or uncle)

or

Stepbrother, stepsister, stepfather, stepmother, son-in-law, daughter-in-law, father-in-law, mother-in-law, brother-in-law, or sister-in-law

or

Any other person (other than your spouse) who lived with you all year as a member of your household if your relationship didn't violate local law. If the person didn't live with you for the required time, see *Exception to time lived with you*, later.

AND

Who wasn't a qualifying child (see Step 1) of any taxpayer for 2023. For this purpose, a person isn't a taxpayer if the person isn't required to file a U.S. income tax return and either doesn't file such a return or files only to get a refund of withheld income tax or estimated tax paid. See Pub. 501 for details and examples.

AND

Who had gross income of less than $4,700 in 2023. If the person was permanently and totally disabled, see *Exception to gross income test*, later.

AND

For whom you provided over half of the person's support in 2023. But see *Children of divorced or separated parents*, *Multiple support agreements*, and *Kidnapped child*, later.

1. Does any person meet the conditions to be your qualifying relative?

☐ **Yes.** Continue ↓   ☐ **No.** (stop)

2. Was your qualifying relative a U.S. citizen, U.S. national, U.S. resident alien, or a resident of Canada or Mexico? (See Pub. 519 for the definition of a U.S. national or U.S. resident alien. If your qualifying relative was adopted, see *Exception to citizen test*, later.)

☐ **Yes.** Continue ↓   ☐ **No.** (stop)
You can't claim this person as a dependent.

3. Was your qualifying relative married?

☐ **Yes.** See *Married person*, later.   ☐ **No.** Continue ↓

4. Are you filing a joint return for 2023?

☐ **Yes.** You can claim this person as a dependent. Complete columns (1) through (3) of the *Dependents* section on page 1 of Form 1040 or 1040-SR. Then, go to Step 5.   ☐ **No.** Continue ↓

5. Could you be claimed as a dependent on someone else's 2023 tax return? (If the person who could claim you on their 2023 tax return is not required to file, and isn't filing a 2023 tax return or is filing a 2023 return only to claim a refund of withheld income tax or estimated tax paid, check "No.") See Steps 1, 2, and 4.

☐ **Yes.** (stop)
You can't claim any dependents. Complete the rest of Form 1040 or 1040-SR and any applicable schedules.   ☐ **No.** You can claim this person as a dependent. Complete columns (1) through (3) of the *Dependents* section on page 1 of Form 1040 or 1040-SR. Then, go to Step 5.

Step 5 Does Your Qualifying Relative Qualify You for the Credit for Other Dependents?

1. Did your qualifying relative have an SSN, ITIN, or ATIN issued on or before the due date of your 2023 return (including extensions)? (Answer "Yes" if you are applying for an ITIN or ATIN for the qualifying relative on or before the return due date (including extensions).)

☐ **Yes.** Continue ↓   ☐ **No.** (stop)
You can't claim the credit for other dependents for this qualifying relative.

2. Was your qualifying relative a U.S. citizen, U.S. national, or U.S. resident alien? (See Pub. 519 for the definition of a U.S. national or a U.S. resident alien. If your qualifying relative was adopted, see *Exception to citizenship test*, later.)

☐ **Yes.** You can claim the credit for other dependents for this dependent. Check the "Credit for other dependents" box in column (4) of the *Dependents* section on page 1 of Form 1040 or 1040-SR for this person.   ☐ **No.** (stop)
You can't claim the credit for other dependents for this qualifying relative.

8. Eliminate the presidential campaign election checkoff to provide $3 by each taxpayer for the campaign funds.

The share of filers who check the box has declined from about 28 percent in 1976 (the first presidential election year for which funds were available) to 4 percent in 2018.

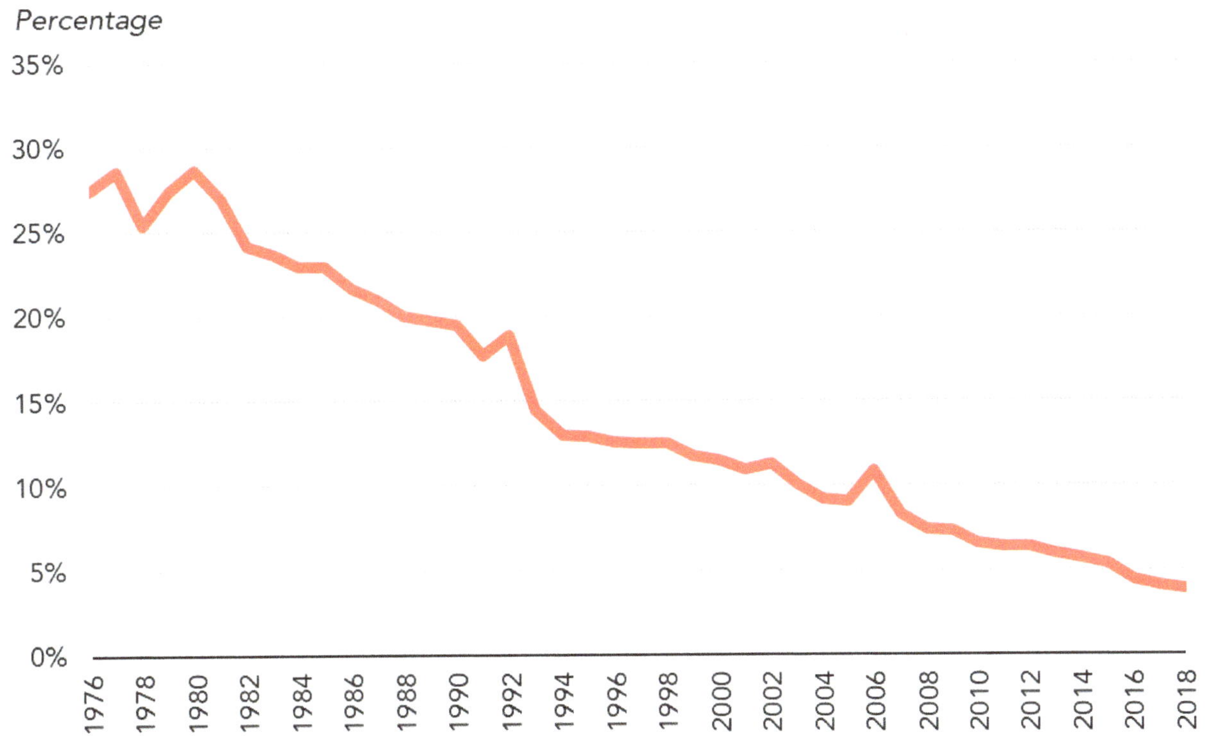

Source: Federal Election Commission (FEC), Presidential Election Campaign Fund Tax Check-Off Chart, April 2019. https://transition.fec.gov/press/bkgnd/presidential_fund.shtml

A taxpayer and the spouse can each check the box at the top of the individual tax form 1040 to elect to have the government transfer $3 each of their tax to the Presidential Election Campaign Fund (PECF). The $3 does not add to their tax bill or reduce their refund. It comes out of the money they paid in taxes and doesn't go to the general fund of the Federal government (maybe, depends, trust but verify, etc.)

This is the only source of funding for the PECF. The funds are meant to provide campaign funds for candidates in the primary and general elections. It was also used for a few years to pay the costs of the parties' presidential conventions. That latter use has been eliminated.

The graph shows the drastic drop off of taxpayers directing the government to put funds in the Presidential Election Fund, down from 28% to 4%.

With the multi-Billion dollar costs of presidential campaigns these days, no major candidate is going to ask for funds from the PECF and accept all the restrictions and limitations imposed by their accepting PECF funds. As a result, John McCain, in 2008, was the last major party candidate to use the PECF.

Lawmakers are aware of the current surplus balance in this fund ($401 Million on 12/31/2023). In 2014 they transferred some of the account to fund $126 Million to pediatric cancer research instead. Look back at the tax form; if you checked the box, it didn't say for pediatric cancer research. That happened because the money was there, and what does Washington tend to do? It follows and, in this case, grabs the money.

Suggestion: Eliminate this one-inch amount of space from the front page of Form 1040. Transfer the funds in the Presidential Election Campaign Fund to the huge unfunded liability "lockbox" of the Social Security and Medicare programs. Look at the section about Social Security in a later chapter. Make this PECF money like the initial deposit we make when we, as individuals, open our own investment accounts.

In fact, that's often what we do when we start to teach our children and grandchildren how to save. We open a savings account and encourage them to watch it grow. Sometimes, they might want to spend it on something they would like to do right now. We hope the idea of saving and paying for what the federal government already owes takes hold.

The same principle applies to our lawmakers. Somehow, they need to appreciate the impending disaster they are setting up if they don't use prudent financial thinking.

We could start here, and maybe we could look at other opportunities in the future not as a new chunk of change to throw at some new idea but as a source of repaying what we already owe.

Another example is the student loan forgiveness program President Biden has undertaken. This is even being done without the checks and balances of the legislative branch. The current estimate of this giveaway to date is a total of $850 Billion of Federal assets. There goes another source to help pay down the unfunded Social Security liabilities. "C'mon man," let's do some clearer thinking here.

One more little thing: there probably is no actual Presidential Election Campaign Fund. The commission reports the balance from time to time. The accounting only shows what came in from the tax return checkoff and what went out in disbursements. If there was actually a fund, wouldn't there be some investment income to add in each year? I saw no reference to say that there is a block of investments comprising the fund. Sounds like another "lockbox," like the social security "lockbox," which doesn't really exist either. See that discussion later in the book.

TIME TO GO OLD FRIEND

9. Eliminate all tax credits.

In recent years, our tax laws have added whole sections of the law to provide tax credits to taxpayers for various types of assistance, reimbursement, or incentives to do one thing or another. There is a difference between tax credits and tax deductions. If you have a $1,000 deduction for a contribution to your IRA account, you reduce your taxable income by $1,000, and if you are in the 12% income tax bracket, you save 12% of $1,000 or $120.

When you receive a retirement savings contribution credit, which allows you a 50% credit for the contribution, you save $500 on your taxes.

The tax deduction reduces your taxable income, and you reduce your tax by the rate of tax you would have paid except for the deduction. The credit actually reduces your income tax by the amount of the credit.

Some of the credits are refundable, and some are not refundable. The refundable credits will pay you even if you have no tax liability against which to apply the credit. That might be considered a negative income tax. The nonrefundable credits will take your tax down to zero, but no further.

The refundable or nonrefundable aspect is one complication of credits.

There are many more complications having to do with whether you are eligible for the credit, and also if you are eligible for the credit but then have income more than is allowable and you are phased out of the credit.

Remember, each credit has its own set of rules as to whether you are eligible for the credit.

Here are most of the credits that need to be considered as a taxpayer prepares their income tax return:

Earned Income Credit

Income limits, Investment income limits, child must meet age 19 or 24 requirements and depends on whether a student or not; child must meet various relationship requirements; you must be a US citizen or resident alien: you and your spouse must be aged 25-64; you must have lived in the US at least s months; special rules for clergy, church employees, and combat pay; The maximum credit for 3 children is $7,830. Refundable. There is an IRS chart after this section that shows the taxpayer how to determine their Earned Income Credit. This is a great exhibit to show how the tax system needs to be simplified.

Child Credit

Must have a qualifying child who is under age 17; subject to phase out with amount of income; child must provide less than half of their support and must have lived with you more than half of the year and be properly claimed as a dependent, dependent can't file a joint return with their spouse; dependent must be a citizen or resident alien; maximum credit per child is $2,000. Partially Refundable and partially Nonrefundable.

Other Child Credit

For a dependent, not a child; subject to income phase-out; maximum credit is $500. Nonrefundable.

Childcare Credit

Dependent must have a social security number; both spouse must work unless spouse is full-time student or is disabled; child must be under age 13. Credits based on a percentage of earned income; maximum of $3,000 for one child and $6,000 for more than one child. Nonrefundable.

Elderly or Disabled Credit

The credit is 15% of an initial amount for example $7,500 initial amount for married filing jointly; initial amount is reduced for pensions and social security benefits and further reduced by one half of the excess of the taxpayers' adjusted gross income over certain amounts, for example, for married filing jointly; the credit is effectively eliminated for married filing jointly with adjusted gross income of $25,000.

American Opportunity Credit

Credit is $2,500 per eligible student pursuing a degree at a four-year higher education: its phases out based on modified adjusted gross income; can be claimed for taxpayer spouse and dependents; must be enrolled at least half time; not have a felony drug conviction: must have SSN, ITIN or ATIN. 40% Refundable.

Lifetime Learning Credit

Credit is 20% of up to $10,000 of qualified education expenses for the enrollment or attendance at an eligible educational institution. Nonrefundable

Adoption Credit

Credit for qualified adoption expense paid or incurred for each eligible child. Maximum credit is $15,950: phases out when modified gross income exceeds $239,230. Nonrefundable.

Other Credits

Retirement Savings Contribution Credit

Mortgage Interest Credit

First-Time Homebuyer Credit for District of Columbia

Alternative Minimum Tax Credit

Health Insurance Premium Assistance Credit

Energy Efficient Home improvement Credit

Residential Clean Energy Credit

Alternative Motor Vehicle Credit

Used Clean Other child credit Vehicle Credit

Alternative Fuel Vehicle Refueling Property Credit

Foreign Tax Credit

This is a best attempt to list most of the credits in the income tax law that can be taken by individual taxpayers as reductions of their income tax liability, with some being allowed in excess of the tax liability (refundable) and some not (nonrefundable).

Most of them have multiple eligibility requirements, none are uniform amongst the credits.

Some of the IRS attempts to explain the requirements are presented below in various flow charts.

This is where the tax law page cutting exercise gets tough. No one wants to take away needed support for any citizen that is living at the lower part of the income ladder. Eliminating the tax credits is what needs to be done. The income tax law needs to return to a tax on income. These tax credits can be replaced with a larger standard deduction and restoring dependent deductions. See the other parts of the book about the standard deduction and dependent deductions. In addition, the Congress needs financial support provided to those in need through social agencies of the government. They shouldn't be burying these non-income tax issues in the income tax law

Business Tax Credits

In addition, there are at least 42 separate credits given to businesses, including:

1. investment credit,
2. work opportunity credit,
3. biofuel producer credit,
4. research credit,
5. low-income housing credit,
6. enhanced oil recovery credit,
7. disabled access credit,
8. renewable electricity production credit,
9. Indian employment credit,
10. FICA tip credit,
11. orphan drug credit,
12. new markets credit,

13. small employer pension plan start-up cost credit,

14. employer-provided childcare facilities and services credit,

15. railroad track maintenance credit,

16. biodiesel and renewable diesel fuels credit,

17. low sulfur diesel fuel production credit,

18. marginal oil and gas production credit,

19. distilled spirits credit,

20. nonconventional source fuel credit,

21. advanced nuclear power facility production credit,

22. energy efficient home credit,

23. energy efficient appliance credit,

24. alternative motor vehicle credit,

25. alternative fuel vehicle refueling property credit,

26. mine rescue team training credit,

27. agricultural chemicals security credit

28. differential wage payment credit,

29. carbon oxide sequestration credit,

30. new lean vehicle credit,

31. qualified plugin electric vehicle credit,

32. small employer health insurance credit,

33. employee retention credit,

34. family and medical leave credit,

35. small employer automatic enrollment credit,

36. sustainable aviation fuel credit,

37. clean hydrogen production credit,

38. commercial clean vehicle credit,

39. advance manufacturing production credit,

40. general credits from an electing large partnership,

41. clean energy production credit,

42. clean fuel production credit.

You can almost see the senators and congresspersons' names attached to some of these favors handed out to their friends and supporters. This whole system of granting favors to businesses needs to be stopped and pulled like a spitting snake from the income tax laws.

If there are legitimate national priorities that must be subsidized, that can be done outside the income tax system. That will occur because of a debate to determine what are national priorities and what are just really favorite causes of those living and being paid in the Swamp.

They all need to be gone as components of the income tax law.

10. Increase the standard deduction to $80,000

Eliminating the myriad of tax credits that have been inserted into the tax law cannot be accomplished if that would hurt those who have benefited from the credits. Even though credit qualifications are complicated and difficult to determine, they do help people with lower incomes provide for their families and help to obtain childcare services.

The higher standard deduction will replace the benefits of the tax credits and will eliminate pages and pages of law and tax return complications. It will be a big wide sweep of the system. The actual amount for the standard deduction can be fine-tuned by authorities such as the Congressional Budget Office. If anything, changes should error on the side of providing an increase in income to the lower-income taxpayers after netting out the tax credits that are eliminated but receiving the benefit of the change upward of the dollar amount of the standard deduction.

Another change that should be made to the standard deduction is to eliminate the phaseout of this standard deduction based on the taxpayer's gross income being above a certain level. This is known as the standard deduction phaseout.

Phaseouts are injected into several parts of the tax law. It's a system that gives on the one hand and then takes back on the other hand. That practice should be stopped. If a deduction or a favorable calculation is a good idea, fair, and reasonable, it should be applicable to all taxpayers. It shouldn't be phased out, making the tax laws even more complicated.

The standard deduction might, for example, be allowed in the following amounts based on the age of the taxpayer and their adjusted gross income:

	Filing As a Single	Filing Jointly
Under age 21	$0	$0
Age 21-25	$20,000	$40,000
Age 26-30	$30,000	$60,000
Over age 30	$40,000	$80,000

Some might say that a taxpayer with taxable income above $500,000 doesn't need an $80,000 standard deduction. Remember, this is part of a total package. This taxpayer will also be subject to increased tax rates, and they will also, as proposed below, lose the deductibility of their state and local taxes, interest expense, medical expenses, and other itemized deductions. It will all work out in the final analysis. Taxpayers will be treated more equally in the application of the income tax law.

11. Eliminate all itemized deductions.

Currently, a taxpayer can elect to take the standard deduction or itemize their deductions. Itemized deductions include medical and dental expenses in excess of 7.5% of the taxpayer's adjusted gross income, state and local taxes with a cap of $10,000, home mortgage interest expense with limits on the amount of the mortgage loan, investment interest expense, charitable contributions, certain casualty losses, and certain miscellaneous expenses.

The TCJA resulted in a 57% reduction in taxpayers choosing to itemize.

Elimination of the itemized deductions will eliminate all of the rules and limits and calculations, not to mention the collection of receipts and support for these deductions. The standard deduction will act as a simple solution to eliminate the itemized deductions and the tax credits noted above.

12. Move investment interest expense from an itemized deduction to a reduction of investment income.

Under current law, investment interest expense is deductible but only as an itemized deduction. Investment interest is interest paid by a taxpayer on debt allocable or incurred to purchase property held for investment, including:

- Property that produces interest, dividends, annuities, or royalties;
- Property that produces gain or loss not derived in the ordinary course of a trade or business from the sale of property.
- An interest in a trade or business.

The deduction for investment interest cannot exceed the taxpayer's investment income.

A simple example would be helpful to illustrate why this type of interest expense should reduce the taxpayer's taxable investment income: A taxpayer borrows $100,000 at 6% interest to buy several stocks to be held in an investment account. The taxpayer pays $6,000 per year in interest expenses and earns $10,000 per year from the investment account. The net investment income is $4,000 and that is the amount that should be taxed.

Rather than treating investment interest expense as an itemized deduction, it should be deducted on the tax return schedule that lists all investment income and thus be treated as a reduction of adjusted gross income.

This would be a correction of the current law that could cause the taxpayer to report the above $10,000 of income but not itemize and not be able to reduce the income by the investment interest expense.

13. Consolidate into one type of account all of the retirement savings programs and education savings programs.

There are several different retirement savings programs that can be used by a taxpayer to set aside funds for retirement. They include different types of IRAs – traditional, Roth, SEP, or Simple as well as the 401K, 403b, and 457 plans.

All of the plans have the same goal: to make saving for retirement attractive in terms of saving taxes from contributions to the plan and earning income in the plan on an income tax-deferred basis.

The number of types of plans should be reduced. In addition, the Roth IRA should be eliminated, grandfathered for plans currently in existence. It seems the main purpose of the Roth is to outsmart the tax law system. Put money in at an advantageous time and avoid taxation on the assets in the account as long as possible. This complicates the tax system and encourages taxpayers to utilize loopholes, sometimes outsmarting themselves but always wasting good time in favor of tax plotting, not planning.

All of the plans should have the same rules, as much as possible, similar limits on contributions across all of the plans, similar rules on distribution requirements and rollovers, similar rules on early distribution and penalties thereon, and similar rules on borrowing from the plan.

Come on, these are retirees. Don't make it difficult, and don't lay traps for those who don't know the complicated rules in this area.

Similar alternate plans exist for education savings programs. It's time to simplify and come up with one plan to help taxpayers save for education.

14. Allow taxpayers who have FICA withholding of less than $1000 to treat that as income tax withheld and reduce income tax.

($1000/.0765 = $13,071 of wages)

That would allow someone earning less than $13,071 in wages to take the $1,000 FICA withholding and apply it as a payment against their income tax, effectively getting a refund for that FICA tax on a low wage earnings.

The income tax rates are progressive in nature, with rates going up with higher income. Unlike income taxes, FICA is a flat tax, meaning the tax rate does not change when income levels change, and everyone pays the same percentage. It's a regressive tax. With taxpayers in the lower income sphere, the FICA tax will be much higher than the income tax. This change will give the taxpayer relief from the regressive nature of the FICA tax.

The employer will continue to pay the employer's 7.65% into the Social Security and Medicare system.

15. Allow the deduction of all charitable contributions as reductions of adjusted gross income.

One of the provisions of the TCJA passed in 2017 was to greatly reduce the use of itemized deductions in personal tax returns. This occurred because of the big increase in the standard deduction from $13,000 to $24,000 for married joint filers, with a similar percentage increase for single and head of household filers.

This, along with the $10,000 cap on the state and local tax itemized deduction, resulted in the total of itemized deductions being less than the increased standard deduction.

Also providing less incentive to make charitable contributions was the provision of the TCJA that lowered tax rates. This made the tax savings for charitable contributions less valuable since the donation would save less income taxes based on a lower tax rate.

The Urban-Brookings Tax Policy Center estimated that "the TCJA reduced the number of households claiming an itemized deduction for their charitable gifts from about 37 million to about 16 million in 2018 and reduced the Federal income tax subsidy for charitable giving by one third – for instance, from about $63 Billion to roughly $42 Billion in 2018." (8)

Interesting to note: The Tax Foundation reported that charitable giving actually increased in 2019 as compared to before the TCJA took effect in 2017. Charitable giving totaled $450 Billion in 2019. (9)

The United States has a strong tradition of supporting charitable organizations. The fact that the TCJA reduced the financial motivation for gifting proves its citizens give for the satisfaction of helping others through the nation's charitable organizations.

The taxpayers in the higher tax brackets also make some of the largest charitable gifts. These taxpayers are not affected by the level of the standard deduction. For example, someone who makes a $10 Million gift to their college is going to itemize in order to obtain that deduction. Those types of gifts will not be affected by the TCJA.

The United States is unique as a country in its support of charitable organizations. In addition, it is important that those organizations do important work in assisting the less fortunate obtain help that may not be available to them on their own or through government help. Charitable organizations do so many things to build a better nation.

It is important to maintain this important sector of our economy and social, healthcare, educational and art and music services. For that reason, this book proposes that charitable contributions should be deducted in the calculation of adjusted gross income before the standard deduction or itemized deductions are deducted. That would enable charitable donors to receive a tax benefit for their giving and still be able to take the standard deduction or itemized deductions.

16. Eliminate the alternative minimum tax.

Do a Google search on the Alternative Minimum Tax. Here is a selection of sources that you will find:

- NBC News; "AMT –the tax we love to hate."
- Charles Schwab: "Nobody enjoys paying taxes, but if you had to pick one tax that is almost universally disliked, it's the AMT."
- Washington Post: "How to calculate the AMT, a tax we love to hate."
- CNBC: "Shedding light on the dreaded AMT."
- Kiplinger: "AMT, the tax we love to hate."
- Wall Street Journal: The hated tax that just won't die."

To mention a few. There's the regular income tax, the gift tax, and the death tax. But when it comes to hated taxes, the prize goes to the AMT calculation of the income tax.

The problem is simple. You go through all of the work of calculating your taxes and preparing your tax returns. You follow the "income tax law." You probably take advantage of the various provisions layered into the law by our well-meaning members of Congress.

You don't pay taxes on tax free municipal bond income; you deduct your allowed state and local taxes; you use the lower capital gain tax rates. You get it all done, and you can live with your answer.

Then you see, you need to do a whole new calculation – the aforementioned and much hated Alternative Minimum Tax. Don't be fooled, it's not an alternative to get you a better answer. No, it was designed to take away those "sinister" tax breaks and loopholes. Which breaks and loopholes? You know, the ones that were created by the members of congress as a part of their ongoing redesign of the "income tax law."

And by the way, the AMT uses different tax rates than the regular income tax rates used in the regular income tax calculation.

Did someone say to never assume the income tax rules are fair and reasonable?

Anyways, here is the worst of the worst. This should be easy to eliminate just because it is hated the most. All that needs to be done is to persuade Congress, "this one has to go."

17. Simplify deprecation

Change all of the depreciation rules so that assets used in a trade or business be divided into their useful life category. There will only be five useful life categories,

    a. 3 years   (example: cars)
    b. 5 years   (example: office equipment and computers)
    c. 10 years   (example: machinery and equipment)
    d. 15 Years   (example: land Improvements like parking lots)
    e. 40 years   (example: buildings)

All of these assets would be depreciated on a straight-line basis, no more double declining, 150% declining, sum of the years' digits, methods of depreciation.

Keep it simple. At the end of all of this jibber dash and mumbo jumbo in the current law, you get to the same answer: all of the cost of each asset is deducted as depreciation by the end of the asset's useful life.

Also, eliminate all bonus depreciation and no section 179 depreciation.

What would this mean in terms of tax rules simplification? IRS Publication 946 spells out 111 pages of information about how to calculate depreciation. The IRS manual states, "The Modified Accelerated Cost Recovery System (MACRS) is used to recover the basis of most business and investment property placed in service after 1986. MACRS consists of two depreciation systems: the General Depreciation System (GDS) and the Alternative Depreciation System (ADS). Generally, these systems provide different methods and recovery periods to use in figuring depreciation deductions.

"This chapter explains how to determine which MACRS depreciation system applies to your property. It also discusses other information you need to know before you can figure depreciation under MACRS. This information includes the property's recovery class, placed in service date, and basis, as well as the applicable recovery period, convention, and depreciation method. It explains how to use this information to figure out your depreciation deduction and how to use a general asset account to depreciate a group of properties.

"MACRS provides three depreciation methods under GDS and one depreciation method under ADS. • The 200% declining balance method over a GDS recovery period. • The 150% declining balance method over a GDS recovery period. • The straight-line method over a GDS recovery period. • The straight-line method over an ADS recovery period."

That almost sounds doable but remember the publication takes 111 pages to explain all of the rules and provides 27 pages of depreciation percentage to deduct over the lives of the assets.

Here is a sampling of the tables that have to be utilized in calculating depreciation:

CHART 5

Appendix A
MACRS Percentage Table Guide
General Depreciation System (GDS)
Alternative Depreciation System (ADS)

Chart 1. *Use this chart to find the correct percentage table to use for any property other than residential rental and nonresidential real property. Use Chart 2 for residential rental and nonresidential real property.*

MACRS System	Depreciation Method	Recovery Period	Convention	Class	Month or Quarter Placed in Service	Table
GDS	200%	GDS/3, 5, 7, 10	Half-Year	3, 5, 7, 10	Any	A-1
GDS	200%	GDS/3, 5, 7, 10	Mid-Quarter	3, 5, 7, 10	1st Qtr 2nd Qtr 3rd Qtr 4th Qtr	A-2 A-3 A-4 A-5
GDS	150%	GDS/3, 5, 7, 10	Half-Year	3, 5, 7, 10	Any	A-14
GDS	150%	GDS/3, 5, 7, 10	Mid-Quarter	3, 5, 7, 10	1st Qtr 2nd Qtr 3rd Qtr 4th Qtr	A-15 A-16 A-17 A-18
GDS	150%	GDS/15, 20	Half-Year	15 & 20	Any	A-1
GDS	150%	GDS/15, 20	Mid-Quarter	15 & 20	1st Qtr 2nd Qtr 3rd Qtr 4th Qtr	A-2 A-3 A-4 A-5
GDS ADS	SL	GDS ADS	Half-Year	Any	Any	A-8
GDS ADS	SL	GDS ADS	Mid-Quarter	Any	1st Qtr 2nd Qtr 3rd Qtr 4th Qtr	A-9 A-10 A-11 A-12
ADS	150%	ADS	Half-Year	Any	Any	A-14
ADS	150%	ADS	Mid-Quarter	Any	1st Qtr 2nd Qtr 3rd Qtr 4th Qtr	A-15 A-16 A-17 A-18

Chart 2. *Use this chart to find the correct percentage table to use for residential rental and nonresidential real property. Use Chart 1 for all other property.*

MACRS System	Depreciation Method	Recovery Period	Convention	Class	Month or Quarter Placed in Service	Table
GDS	SL	GDS/27.5	Mid-Month	Residential Rental	Any	A-6
GDS	SL SL	GDS/31.5 GDS/39	Mid-Month	Nonresidential Real	Any	A-7 A-7a
ADS	SL	ADS/30	Mid-Month	Residential Rental	Any	A-13
	SL	ADS/40	Mid-Month	Residential Rental and Nonresidential Real	Any	A-13a

Chart 3. **Income Inclusion Amount Rates for MACRS Leased Listed Property**

	Table
Amount A Percentages	A-19
Amount B Percentages	A-20

39

CHART 6

Table A-10. (Continued)

Year	\multicolumn{13}{c}{Recovery periods in years}

Year	18	19	20	22	24	25	26.5	28	30	35	40	45	50
1	3.47%	3.29%	3.125%	2.841%	2.604%	2.5%	2.358%	2.232%	2.083%	1.786%	1.563%	1.389%	1.25%
2	5.56	5.26	5.000	4.545	4.167	4.0	3.774	3.571	3.333	2.857	2.500	2.222	2.00
3	5.56	5.26	5.000	4.545	4.167	4.0	3.774	3.571	3.333	2.857	2.500	2.222	2.00
4	5.56	5.26	5.000	4.545	4.167	4.0	3.774	3.571	3.333	2.857	2.500	2.222	2.00
5	5.55	5.26	5.000	4.546	4.167	4.0	3.774	3.571	3.333	2.857	2.500	2.222	2.00
6	5.56	5.26	5.000	4.545	4.167	4.0	3.774	3.572	3.333	2.857	2.500	2.222	2.00
7	5.55	5.26	5.000	4.546	4.167	4.0	3.774	3.571	3.333	2.857	2.500	2.222	2.00
8	5.56	5.26	5.000	4.545	4.167	4.0	3.773	3.572	3.333	2.857	2.500	2.222	2.00
9	5.55	5.27	5.000	4.546	4.167	4.0	3.774	3.571	3.333	2.857	2.500	2.222	2.00
10	5.56	5.26	5.000	4.545	4.167	4.0	3.773	3.572	3.333	2.857	2.500	2.222	2.00
11	5.55	5.27	5.000	4.546	4.166	4.0	3.774	3.571	3.333	2.857	2.500	2.222	2.00
12	5.56	5.26	5.000	4.545	4.167	4.0	3.773	3.572	3.334	2.857	2.500	2.222	2.00
13	5.55	5.27	5.000	4.546	4.166	4.0	3.774	3.571	3.333	2.857	2.500	2.222	2.00
14	5.56	5.26	5.000	4.545	4.167	4.0	3.773	3.572	3.334	2.857	2.500	2.222	2.00
15	5.55	5.27	5.000	4.546	4.166	4.0	3.774	3.571	3.333	2.857	2.500	2.222	2.00
16	5.56	5.26	5.000	4.545	4.167	4.0	3.773	3.572	3.334	2.857	2.500	2.222	2.00
17	5.55	5.27	5.000	4.546	4.166	4.0	3.774	3.571	3.333	2.857	2.500	2.222	2.00
18	5.56	5.26	5.000	4.545	4.167	4.0	3.773	3.572	3.334	2.857	2.500	2.222	2.00
19	2.08	5.27	5.000	4.546	4.166	4.0	3.774	3.571	3.333	2.857	2.500	2.222	2.00
20		1.97	5.000	4.545	4.167	4.0	3.773	3.572	3.334	2.857	2.500	2.222	2.00
21			1.875	4.546	4.166	4.0	3.774	3.571	3.333	2.857	2.500	2.222	2.00
22				4.545	4.167	4.0	3.773	3.572	3.334	2.857	2.500	2.222	2.00
23				1.705	4.166	4.0	3.774	3.571	3.333	2.857	2.500	2.222	2.00
24					4.167	4.0	3.773	3.572	3.334	2.857	2.500	2.222	2.00
25					1.562	4.0	3.774	3.571	3.333	2.857	2.500	2.222	2.00
26						1.5	3.773	3.572	3.334	2.857	2.500	2.222	2.00
27							3.302	3.571	3.333	2.857	2.500	2.223	2.00
28								3.572	3.334	2.858	2.500	2.222	2.00
29								1.339	3.333	2.857	2.500	2.223	2.00
30									3.334	2.858	2.500	2.222	2.00
31									1.250	2.857	2.500	2.223	2.00
32										2.858	2.500	2.222	2.00
33										2.857	2.500	2.223	2.00
34										2.858	2.500	2.222	2.00
35										2.857	2.500	2.223	2.00
36										1.072	2.500	2.222	2.00
37											2.500	2.223	2.00
38											2.500	2.222	2.00
39											2.500	2.223	2.00
40											2.500	2.222	2.00
41											0.937	2.223	2.00
42												2.222	2.00
43												2.223	2.00
44												2.222	2.00
45												2.223	2.00
46												0.833	2.00
47–50													2.00
51													0.75

There it is - MACRS using GDS and ADS in only 28 pages of tables, to be used for each asset each year. Some companies have whole departments of accountants to maintain depreciation schedules and compute depreciation.

It can be much simpler. Provide for only five lives, for short-life, mid-life, and long-term life assets. Allow only straight-line depreciation, no double declining, and no 150 declining. Compute depreciation in the first year of an asset by assuming a half-year depreciation in the first year with no mid-month or mid-quarter conventions.

The IRS publication also says, "You can elect to recover all or part of the cost of certain qualifying property, up to a limit, by deducting it in the year you place the property in service. This is the section 179 deduction. You can elect the section 179 deduction instead of recovering the cost by taking depreciation deductions."

This extra way of writing off depreciable assets was added many years ago, and like many new provisions, it started out small, allowing an annual write-off of $10,000. In 2023, the allowed write-off is $1,160,000. It grew in size and complication with an additional provision that can reduce the deduction to zero. Here is how the IRS explains it: "If the cost of your qualifying section 179 property placed in service in a year is more than $2,890,000, you must generally reduce the dollar limit (but not below zero) by the amount of cost over $2,890,000. If the cost of your section 179 property placed in service during 2023 is $4,050,000 or more, you cannot take a section 179 deduction."

Not content with just multiple methods and conventions, and including the Section 179, "Special Deal," the law also added provisions allowing bonus depreciation. Per Publication 946, "You can take a special depreciation allowance to recover part of the cost of qualified property (defined next) placed in service during the tax year. The allowance applies only for the first year you place the property in service. The allowance is an additional deduction you can take after any section 179 deduction and before you figure regular depreciation under MACRS for the year you place the property in service."

Looks like the fruits and nuts lobbyists got this one through, as the definition of qualified property is: "Your property is qualified property if it is one of the following.

• Qualified reuse and recycling property.

• Certain qualified property acquired after September 27, 2017.

• Certain plants bearing fruits and nuts."

These provisions were meant to be a stimulus provision and allowed for 100% write-off in years 2017-2022 and then reducing percentages through 2026.

Needless to say, there are pages and pages of ifs, ands, and buts to complicate the giveaway.

Calculation of depreciation would be greatly simplified by tossing the 111 pages of complicated rules and inserting one paragraph as follows:

Depreciation is calculated on a straight-line basis over the useful life of the asset, allowing for a half-year depreciation in the first year.

There it is, goodbye to all those accountants toiling in the back rooms tracking all of the fixed assets and all of the calculations of depreciation. Good-bye to all of the fruit and nut lobbyists and their brethren getting special breaks. Good-bye to all of the hours spent by tax return preparers to calculate depreciation using this byzantine complex of rules, giveaways, and take backs.

We get the same answer as to the taxes being collected. We just eliminate untold amounts of effort to get there. Also, no small favor; we simplify and make everything more understandable. "Special Bonus" (as they say in the tax code), businesses have a clear set of rules and no changes up and down from year to year.

18. Eliminate depreciation recapture on sales of property

The tax law has a particularly two-faced section of the law which is called depreciation recapture. Thinking about all the gyrations a taxpayer has to go through to initially calculate depreciation (discussed immediately above), we now come to depreciation recapture.

It turns out they really didn't mean to give the taxpayer a bunch of different ways to calculate depreciation and to encourage the taxpayer to choose the methods that gave the taxpayer the highest tax deduction. Or, maybe they did, and then they didn't.

When the taxpayer sells a depreciable capital asset and receives a price that results in a gain when compared to the cost basis of the property, which is also being reduced by the depreciation previously taken – then the gain really isn't capital gain after all. Any depreciation taken, in some cases, or depreciation taken in excess of straight-line depreciation, is recaptured and taxed as ordinary income.

Along with the simplification of the calculation of depreciation, the tax reforms should eliminate the recapture of the depreciation that was allowed to the taxpayer in previous years.

19. Collision Course

The U. S. has an overly complicated income tax system, built over 110 years of one change after another, to meet revenue needs and fulfill politicians' promises to the American public. That alone requires immediate and urgent attention. But there's also the matter of the multi Trillion-dollar anchor pulling down the country's fiscal ship. That anchor is the underfunded future costs of the Social Security and Medicare systems.

Let's talk about the stewardship of the Social Security system. Where do the taxes collected for Social Security and Medicare go within the Federal government? In a presidential debate against George W. Bush, Al Gore told the nation, "I will keep Social Security in an ironclad lockbox." In fact, there is no lock box of funds being held to pay out future Social Security benefits.

George W. Bush stated the truth in 2005 when he said: "A lot of people in America think there is a trust – that we take your money in payroll taxes and then we hold it for you, and then when you retire, we give it back to you. But there is no trust fund, just IOU's."

Bush was right. There is an accounting of the Social Security funds but no trust account holding marketable securities. The government takes in Social Security and Medicare taxes, pays out benefits, and then accounts for the excess in an accounting record. However, the excess funds that are collected each year are used by the government to pay other government expenses. The government does issue non-marketable agreements (IOUs) agreeing to pay back the money and even accrue some interest due.

But compare this system to a corporation with a pension plan for its employees. It would be like the corporation collecting contributions from its employees or agreeing to contribute corporate funds for a 401K plan but then not investing those monies. Instead, it would issue IOUs to the 401K plan and use the retirement plan's money to fund the business. Guess what? In the private enterprise world, that is totally illegal. In the Federal government world, it is what is happening to the Social Security system's taxes and revenues.

No lock box ever existed. And there is no Trust Fund holding $3.2 Trillion of Social Security contributions, interest and also the income taxes charged to retirees that paid income taxes on their Social Security benefits. All there is an accounting of what has come in and what has gone out in benefits, and what has gone into the government's regular spending. There are also some file cabinets full of IOUs from the US Treasury that are not marketable and are only pieces of paper saying what is owed.

The situation is actually much worse than the example given above about how the Social Security funds are borrowed by the government but would never happen with a corporate pension fund. That would be a big no-no for any corporation to borrow from a pension fund that was established for the corporation's employees.

With Social Security, we have to remember where the funds going into the system are coming from. None of it comes from the government. Unlike a corporation which pays for all of a pension plan for its employees and/or matches employee contributions into a 401K plan, the government puts no money into the Social Security pension system. As noted, the government takes out the funds to pay general Federal spending. It puts nothing into the plan to pay for part of the Social Security pensions promised to all who worked and contributed.

When a bank, stockbroker, or other fiduciary holds the corporation's pension investments or 401K plan investments, they serve as a fiduciary, as a custodian holding the corporation retirement plan's investments. That is basically what the Federal government is doing for Social Security contributions. Never would a fiduciary acting as a custodian for retirement plan assets be able to take funds from those accounts and use the money for paying their own operating expenses. How does the Federal government justify doing that? They only answer has to be the old saw: "That's how it's always been done."

Maybe so, but this is really bad.

The Social Security system is keeping track of the wrong numbers. It should be concentrating on the future obligations of the Social Security and Medicare plans. It should determine the present value of those obligations. It should establish a plan to pay down the underfunded obligations, pay down those obligations, and hold those funds in a separate trust account.

In the "Financial Report of the United States Government Fiscal 2023" issued by Janet L. Yellen, Secretary of the Treasury, on February 15, 2024 — in that report, the future obligations and the present values of the unfunded liabilities are reported. There is no good news here. The report states that the present value of future obligations, net of future revenues, for Social Security and Medicare is $78,400,000,000,000 ($78.4 Trillion).

Against that amount of liability, the "Trust Fund" holds $3.2 Trillion dollars of assets. Of course, the "Trust Fund" is a loosely worded term. It is a bunch of file cabinets holding IOUs from the Federal government. They carry a government-computed interest rate. The interest rate paid in 2022 was 2.4%, according to the 2023 annual report of the Board of Trustees.

The 2.4% rate paid by the Federal government to the Social Security "fund' compares to the 3.29% rate paid by the U. S. Treasury to the holders of U. S. Treasury long-term 20-year bonds. A 27% discount off of the going rate for marketable U. S. Treasury bonds sounds like an inside deal for what the government pays for the money it owes to Social Security for non-marketable IOU slips of paper.

One argument put forth for this system is that to invest the funds in actual U. S. Treasury bonds would remove $3.2 trillion from the economy. That, of course, is not true.   What it would actually do is put real hard assets up (U. S. Treasury bonds) as assets to pay for future benefits for the Social Security and Medicare participants,

Once those assets are set side in a true trust fund, then future employee and employer contributions and future investment income collections would be deposited into the fund. Payments for benefits being paid out would come out of the fund in transfers to the Social Security system. Money that comes in each year that is in excess of benefits that are paid out would stay in this trust fund and be invested.

President George W. Bush, during his term of office, floated the possibility that some of the Social Security and Medicare assets would be invested in the stock market. Is that crazy? Of course not. His suggestion was to give taxpayers an option for each of their individual social security accounts.

In the 2000 Presidential campaign, George Bush's website described his Social Security reform plan as follows:

"But to save Social Security for the next generation, he will lead a bipartisan effort to reform it by giving individuals the option of voluntarily investing a portion of their Social Security payroll taxes in personal retirement accounts. These accounts will earn higher rates of return and generate wealth that can be owned and passed on from parents to their children."

Our proposal is not the same proposal as was made by President Bush. He envisioned separate accounts for each Social Security recipient, each with the authority to shift investments into the stock market.

This proposal, on the other hand, is to manage the investments held by the Social Security program in the same way that all corporate pension plan or 401K plan assets are managed.

Almost every other retirement fund, endowment fund, and trust fund in the United States follows a detailed investment policy that invests the funds' assets in an allocation of fixed income and stock market investments. Such an investment policy is considered the most prudent and results in a higher return than any fund that strictly invests in fixed-income securities, let alone fixed-income non-marketable IOUs, with interest rates determined by the debtor, the Federal government.

The total of the United States stock market is estimated to be valued at $50.8 Trillion on January 1, 2024. Investing half of the trust fund, or about $1.5 Trillion, would not cause the market to go up like a rocket (as some have suggested) from too many dollars chasing too few stocks. Not at all. It is just 3% of the current market. In fact, it will provide more support for the stocks and, in the long term, could have a longer-term positive effect on the market, the trust fund, and even on the other retirement funds, investment accounts, and endowment funds in the country.

Walling off the Social Security and Medicare funds from other government spending might cause some effort to replace those funds. That might instill more discipline in the expenditure of funds for the government, and it might cause the government to seriously evaluate the debt levels and the future obligations to the Social Security and Medicare beneficiaries and start to raise questions like if we decide to implement this next new idea, where will the money come from. It might even pull the government's ostrich head out of the sand.

It would certainly be the right thing to do and stop the non-fiduciary ways the current program is run. It's time to start getting serious about the future retirements of our citizens.

IRC 7501 provides that whenever any person is required to collect or withhold any internal revenue taxes from any other person and to pay over such tax to the United States, the amount of the tax shall be held in a special trust fund for the United States. Trust fund taxes include employment taxes and certain types of excise taxes.

The Trust Fund Recovery Penalty (TFRP) is authorized by IRC 6672(a), which states:

> *"Any person required to collect, truthfully account for, and pay over any tax imposed by this title who willfully fails to collect such tax, or truthfully account for and pay over such tax, or willfully attempts in any manner to evade or defeat any such tax on the payment thereof, shall, in addition to other penalties provided by law, be liable to a penalty equal to the total amount of the tax evaded, or not collected, or not accounted for and paid over.*

It seems highly hypocritical to penalize a corporate officer for not holding withheld payroll taxes in trust and then not remitting them to the IRS. When those funds are received by the government, there is no trust fund. The money is essentially merged with all the other money in the government and even spent on general government expenditures in exchange for unmarketable government IOUs. How is this fair? Oh, I forgot the statement of my former boss: "Don't assume the income tax law (and the payroll tax law) is fair."

20. We need help

It seems that the Federal Government is run by some highly qualified people. The Senate and the House have a bunch of people who are highly qualified to understand basic financial information. Yet, the government continues to be run in a way that suggests there is never a day of reckoning. Do our leaders never look at a balance sheet?

Do they not understand that the government is overloaded with debt and unfunded Social Security and Medicare obligations? It seems like as long as revenues plus borrowings exceed expenditures, everything is fine. BUT don't the borrowings have to be paid back? Won't the interest on the outstanding debt start to eat a bigger chunk of the available cash inflow? When will this charade come to a screeching halt?

Some report or some method of bringing the balance sheet to bear on the minds of those who run the government has to be created. Red lights are flashing, but right now, for some reason, no one sees them.

In the conclusion of the 2023 Annual Report of the Board of Trustees of the Social Security Funds, the trustees made the following comments:

"Under the intermediate assumptions, the projected hypothetical combined OASI and DI Trust Fund asset reserves become depleted and unable to pay scheduled benefits in full on a timely basis in 2034. At the time of depletion of these combined reserves, continuing income to the combined trust funds would be sufficient to pay 80 percent of scheduled benefits. The OASI Trust Fund reserves are projected to become depleted in 2033, at which time OASI income would be sufficient to pay 77 percent of OASI scheduled benefits. DI Trust Fund asset reserves are not projected to become depleted during the 75-year period ending in 2097. Lawmakers have a broad continuum of policy options that would close or reduce Social Security's long-term financing shortfall.

Estimates for many such policy options are available at ssa.gov/OACT/solvency/provisions/.

The Trustees recommend that lawmakers address the projected trust fund shortfalls in a timely way in order to phase in necessary changes gradually and give workers and beneficiaries time to adjust to them. Implementing changes sooner rather than later would allow more generations to share in the needed revenue increases or reductions in scheduled benefits. Social Security will play a critical role in the lives of 67 million beneficiaries and 180 million covered workers and their families during 2023. With informed discussion, creative thinking, and timely legislative action, Social Security can continue to protect future generations."

Notice the report above comes from the "Trustees" of the "Trust Funds." There are no funds in a trust. There is no trust. It appears the Trustees are asleep in the control room.

We would also add it's time to protect those funds from invasion by the government, and it's also high time to utilize modern investment theory. It's time not to invest solely in discounted U. S Treasury obligations, and it's time to require an allocation of funds between diversified fixed-income obligations and a diversified mix of investment in the total stock market. Put the hand cuffs on the government and take them off of the taxpayers.

We have to shift from an attitude of what's important right now to an understanding of what is going to happen in the future. It's basic common sense. We have to build our understanding and our reaction to this growing Federal debt problem.

21. Eliminate income taxation of Social Security benefits

Let's get back to rebuilding our income tax laws.

Isn't it disheartening that taxpayers are taxed on their wages their whole lives in order to receive Social Security checks after their retirement age? Their benefits are earned by taxing income in their preretirement years.

But ever since 1984, their Social Security checks have been treated as taxable income and taxed a second time. This change in the treatment of the Social Security benefits was the recommendation of the Greenspan Commission on Social Security Reform in 1983.

The new law taxed 50% of Social Security benefits, but once the taxability of benefits was established, as so many other times have happened, the law was changed in 1993 to tax 85% of Social Security benefits.

Also, through the history of Social Security, the rate of taxes paid by employees and employers has increased substantially. When taxes were first collected in 1937, employees and employers each paid 1% or a total of 2% on the first $3,000 of wages. Today, the rate each employee and employer pays is 7.65% or a total of 15.3% on the first $168,600 of wages. Those have become big numbers considering, for example, in 2020 over 65 Million taxpayers had an average effective income tax rate of 1.5% or less. 15.3% is ten times larger than the income tax for these 65 Million taxpayers.

The net effect of now taxing Social Security pensions is that the benefits that are paid out by the Social Security system are partially taken back by the Internal Revenue Service. How does it make sense to pay out benefits to retirees from one pocket and then take the money back via a tax on 85% of the benefits that were paid? Because the benefits are coming out of Social Security and the income tax is going back to the IRS, those dollars are on a long road trip from one big building in Washington D.C., to another big building in the same town. Come on, if you are going to steal from Peter to pay Paul, just call up and ask; you don't have to run every check around the whole 3.9 Million square miles comprising the United States.

The bottom-line effect of taxing the benefits is to reduce the benefit, net of income taxes. This way, the reduction in monthly benefits is never highlighted. It happens, but nobody realizes it. Once again, "the liars are doing the figuring."IRS Publication 17 is entitled "Federal Income Taxes for Individuals." It is the 140-page booklet of instructions on how to file your tax return. Regarding determining whether your Social Security benefits are taxable, it says, "to find out whether any of your benefits may be taxable, compare the base amount (explained later) for your filing status with the total of:

    1. One-half of your benefits; plus

    2. All your other income, including tax-exempt interest.

"Exclusions. When making this comparison, don't reduce your other income by any exclusions for: • Interest from qualified U.S. savings bonds, • Employer-provided adoption benefits, • Interest on education loans, • Foreign earned income or foreign housing, or • Income earned by bona fide residents of American Samoa or Puerto Rico.

"Figuring total income. To figure the total of one-half of your benefits plus your other income, use Worksheet 7-1, discussed later. If the total is more than your base amount, part of your benefits may be taxable. If you are married and file a joint return for the year, you and your spouse must combine your incomes and your benefits to figure whether any of your combined benefits are taxable. Even if your spouse didn't receive any benefits, you must add your spouse's income to yours to figure whether any of your benefits are taxable."

This is just one example of how every change in the calculation of a tax return adds to the complexity of the process. It's also an example of what my first boss told me when I started to work as a CPA right out of college: "Never assume the tax law is fair." That one stuck with me. He was right.

22. Changes in treatment of capital gains and losses.

Gains on the sale of capital assets held less than one year are currently treated as ordinary income and taxed at regular rates.

Gains on the sale of capital assets held for more than one year are taxed at lower "capital gain' rates.

Net capital losses are deductible but only at the rate of $3,000 per year. Capital losses are netted against capital gains to calculate a net capital loss.

The IRS guidebook describes the treatment of capital gains and losses as follows:

> "Almost everything you own and use for personal or investment purposes is a capital asset. Examples of capital assets include a home, personal-use items like household furnishings, and stocks or bonds held as investments. When you sell a capital asset, the difference between the adjusted basis in the asset and the amount you realized from the sale is a capital gain or a capital loss. Generally, an asset's basis is its cost to the owner, but if you received the asset as a gift or inheritance, refer to Publication 551, Basis of Assets for information about your basis. You have a capital gain if you sell the asset for more than your adjusted basis. You have a

capital loss if you sell the asset for less than your adjusted basis. Losses from the sale of personal-use property, such as your home or car, aren't tax deductible.

"Short-term or long-term

"To correctly arrive at your net capital gain or loss, capital gains and losses are classified as long-term or short-term. Generally, if you hold the asset for more than one year before you dispose of it, your capital gain or loss is long-term. If you hold it one year or less, your capital gain or loss is short-term. For exceptions to this rule, such as property acquired by gift, property acquired from a decedent, or patent property, refer to Publication 544, Sales and Other Dispositions of Assets; for commodity futures, see Publication 550, Investment Income and Expenses; or for applicable partnership interests, see Publication 541, Partnerships. To determine how long you held the asset, you generally count from the day after the day you acquired the asset up to and including the day you disposed of the asset.

"If you have a net capital gain, a lower tax rate may apply to the gain than the tax rate that applies to your ordinary income. The term "net capital gain" means the amount by which your net long-term capital gain for the year is more than your net short-term capital loss for the year. The term "net long-term capital gain" means long-term capital gains reduced by long-term capital losses including any unused long-term capital loss carried over from previous years. The term "net short-term capital loss" means the excess of short-term capital losses (including any unused short-term capital losses carried over from previous years) over short-term capital gains for the year.

"Capital gains tax rates

"Net capital gains are taxed at different rates depending on overall taxable income, although some or all net capital gain may be taxed at 0%. For taxable years beginning in 2023, the tax rate on most net capital gain is no higher than 15% for most individuals.

"A capital gains rate of 0% applies if your taxable income is less than or equal to:

- $44,625 for single and married filing separately;

- $89,250 for married filing jointly and qualifying surviving spouse; and

- $59,750 for head of household.

"A capital gains rate of 15% applies if your taxable income is:

- more than $44,625 but less than or equal to $492,300 for single;

- more than $44,625 but less than or equal to $276,900 for married filing separately;

- more than $89,250 but less than or equal to $553,850 for married filing jointly and qualifying surviving spouse; and

- more than $59,750 but less than or equal to $523,050 for head of household.

However, a capital gains rate of 20% applies to the extent that your taxable income exceeds the thresholds set for the 15% capital gain rate.

"There are a few other exceptions where capital gains may be taxed at rates greater than 20%:

1. The taxable part of a gain from selling section 1202 qualified small business stock is taxed at a maximum 28% rate.

2. Net capital gains from selling collectibles (such as coins or art) are taxed at a maximum 28% rate.

3. The portion of any unrecaptured section 1250 gain from selling section 1250 real property is taxed at a maximum 25% rate.

"Note: Net short-term capital gains are subject to taxation as ordinary income at graduated tax rates.

"Limit on the deduction and carryover of losses.

"If your capital losses exceed your capital gains, the amount of the excess loss that you can claim to lower your income is the lesser of $3,000 ($1,500 if married filing separately) or your total net loss shown on line 16 of Schedule D (Form 1040), Capital Gains and Losses."

Hope you enjoyed reading about capital gains and losses in the above section. It is just a taste of how it is explained in the IRS manual.

Here is a brief history of the capital gain rate calculations written by Realized Financial, Inc. in December 2020:

Creating The Capital Gains Tax

"Why did the capital gains tax come into being? What was the government's motivation?

"After WWI, the Republicans took victory in the 1920 Federal elections. They passed the Revenue Act of 1921. This act began the capital gains tax. Andrew Mellon, Secretary of the Treasury, pushed for lower taxes to help the economy expand. These tax reductions played a role in jump-starting the roaring 20's.

"Right after the act was instituted, the capital gains tax rate was set at 12.5%, although Mellon wanted an even lower rate. Unlike our current long-term capital gains tax, the 1921 tax applied to assets held for at least two years.

Capital Gains Taxes During The 20th Century

"Following the Great Depression, the capital gains tax rate jumped to 23%. It then fell to 15% briefly at the beginning of WWI. In 1942, the tax went back up, hitting a new high of 25%. From here, it would go on to make a long run across a high plateau, peaking at 35% during the mid-1970s. It would finally fall back to 15% but not until 2003.

"Since 2003, the capital gains tax rate hasn't gone above 20%. The long-term rate hit a low of 5% between 2003-2007. It trended to its lowest point during the 2008-2012 period, hitting zero for the lower bound rate. Three different rates were introduced during the 2008-2012 period. The 0% rate applied to the 10%- and 15%-income tax brackets. The other two rates were 15% (25%, 28%, and 33% brackets) and 20% for those in the 38.6% and above bracket.

"When President Trump was elected in 2016, he reduced the number of long-term capital gains tax brackets from seven to only three. These changes went into effect starting with the 2018 tax year and have been there ever since.

"Most investors strive to hold investment property for more than a year to achieve long-term capital gains status and take advantage of the tax break. Throughout history, long-term capital gains rates have fluctuated but have remained below ordinary income (and thus short-term capital gains) rates, showing that it does pay to be patient."

What needs to be changed?

In this book, we are looking at income tax simplification, consistency, and fairness.

The treatment of capital gains can be simplified, made consistent with the treatment of other income, and made fairer by not distinguishing between long or short-term or gain or loss.

Capital gains should be taxed at the same rate as other income, whether long or short gains. Capital losses should be fully deductible in the year of loss, with no $3,000 limitation.

The current law also includes a stratification of dividends.

23. How about Qualified dividends?

Most dividends from U. S. companies are considered Qualified Dividends. There are exceptions, of course. Qualified dividends do not include dividends by real estate investment trusts or money market accounts.

Qualified and ordinary dividends have different tax implications. The tax rate is 0% on qualified dividends if taxable income is less than $44,625 for singles and $89,250 for joint-married filers in the tax year 2023.

Single filers who make more than $44,625 or $89,250 jointly have a 15% tax rate on qualified dividends. For those with income that exceeds $492,300 for a single person or $553,850 for a married couple, the capital gains tax rate is 20%.

There is an additional 3.8% tax on investment income if the taxpayer has adjusted gross income over a threshold amount.

A shareholder must buy a stock before the ex-dividend date and hold it for more than 60 days during a certain period in order for the dividend to be qualified. There are other holding period rules for preferred stocks and mutual fund shares.

The reform called for in this book would tax dividends in the same way as all other ordinary income. The separate calculations for qualified dividends would be eliminated. Poof, there goes several pages of complicated tax rules.

24. Eliminate Carried Interest

Here's a part of the income tax law that you hear mentioned whenever tax reform gets talked about, but it's always been a part of the tax law that survives. Each time all the tax reform smoke clears, there stands Carried Interest.

Most taxpayers don't even know what carried interest is, let alone care about where to report it on their tax return.

They should be so lucky. There are very few taxpayers that get to report carried interest, but oh boy, those that do are doing very, very well. Maybe so well that they somehow fight off the tax reformers every time. You have to wonder how that works.

So, a short lesson on what carried interest is, and why you probably never receive any. Carried interest is the share of profits received by the general partners of hedge funds, venture capital funds, and private equity funds.

Who invests in those kinds of investments, basically only the richest of the rich. In fact, the investors in those funds are so rich they don't mind paying the general partners 20% of their returns from the investments in the funds. That 20% fee is what the mysterious carried interest income is.

Someone else manages a group of fast-food restaurants for some investors; that person gets paid a salary and a bonus. Some brilliant software engineer/manager manages some projects for a software company, and if it hits big with some of the new software that is developed. That manager gets paid a salary and a bonus and maybe some stock options. A trust department investment manager manages a portfolio of stocks and bonds in the trust department for the various trust customers. That person gets paid a salary and a bonus.

Here's the difference: everyone except the hedge fund managers reports their compensation as ordinary income, salary, and wages paid to them by their employer. Not the hedge fund managers. They report their income as carried interest. That does not get taxed as ordinary income, but instead, it gets taxed as long-term capital gains.

Remember what my boss told me many years ago, "the first thing that you have to know is that the income tax law is not fair." Once again, he was right.

The managers who are not hedge fund managers noted above will pay up to a maximum income tax rate of 38.8%. The hedge fund manager pays the maximum capital gains tax rate of 20% plus the 3.8% investment income tax rate. Thus, a hedge fund manager making $100,000,000 a year pays a tax of $23,800,000, not the $40,800,000 that would be paid if the hedge fund manager paid the same rate of taxes as most people.

Sound like a sweet deal? It is, in fact, it's so sweet it's very sour to the taste of every taxpayer not a hedge fund manager.

Carried interest has to go.

25. Eliminate tax exemption for interest income from state and local government borrowings.

The Tax Foundation wrote a very extensive review of this area in an article written by Scott Greenberg, dated July 21, 2016.

Here are some of the points made in that article:

1. "Since the enactment of the federal income in 1913, interest on state and local bonds has been excluded from taxation. However, the original reason for this exclusion – concern about the constitutionality of taxing the borrowing power of state and local governments – is likely no longer applicable.

2. The strongest economic justification for the municipal bonds tax exemption is that it encourages state and local governments to invest in infrastructure projects that create benefits for nonresidents. On the other hand, there is also reason to believe that the tax exemption will cause municipalities to overinvest in infrastructure, particularly if states and localities are also able to shift their tax burdens onto nonresidents.

3. A tax exclusion is a policy designed for subsidizing state and local debt. It delivers larger benefits for taxpayers in higher income brackets, shuts some investors completely out of the municipal bond market, and makes the subsidy difficult for Congress and voters to evaluate.

4. Most importantly, there is a compelling case that the current tax treatment of municipal bond interest is inefficient. For every dollar that the federal government forgoes due to the provision, state and local governments receive less than a dollar in lower borrowing costs; the remainder goes largely to high-income households."

It was estimated that this exemption from taxation would cost the Federal government $617 Billion over the ten-year period from 2017-2026.

The paper was quite extensive in its analysis and, in the end, came to the following conclusions:

1. "Like almost every provision in the tax code, the tax exemption for municipal bond interest has many passionate defenders.
2. "In this paper, I have tried to highlight some of the shortcomings of the current tax treatment of municipal bond interest. While intended as a subsidy for state and local infrastructure spending that benefits nonresidents, the exclusion of municipal bond interest also applies to many state and local spending projects that do not need to be subsidized.
3. "The provision is designed poorly, delivering larger benefits for taxpayers in higher income brackets, and shutting some investors completely out of the municipal bond market.
4. "Finally, the subsidy is inefficient, as only a portion of every dollar forgone by the federal government ends up in the hands of state and local governments.
5. "This evidence points to a clear takeaway: no provision in the U.S. tax code should be 'sacrosanct.' The U.S. tax code is badly in need of reform, and any tax reform effort will need to limit or eliminate tax expenditures in order to broaden the federal tax base. As Congress moves forward with discussions about tax reform, it should keep every tax provision on the table, including the exclusion of municipal bond interest."

I inserted the information from this paper in the book because it did an excellent job of analysis, and the conclusions parallel the thrust of the book: namely, that this provision of the income tax law, and so many other provisions need to be eliminated and a much simpler income tax law (remember the definition of an income tax law is a tax on income, not a law with income tax and a thousand other themes and causes) needs to be the replacement for what we have.

Giving a $617 Billion subsidy to state and local governments in a section of the income tax code hides that information and policy from the budgeting process and the public.

26. Eliminate passive loss limitations on real estate investments and other passive activities.

The provisions to limit passive losses have been in the tax law since 1986, with the purpose being to prevent taxpayers from using depreciation deductions to create a tax loss, which would be used to reduce other taxable income.

Passive losses arise from real estate rental activity even if the owner is actively involved in the management as well as other business activities in which the owner is not actively involved. There are definitions of what active involvement is. In addition, a real estate professional, also defined in the law, is allowed to deduct losses from real estate activities.

If the taxpayer or the spouse participated in a passive rental real estate activity, the amount of the loss that is disallowed is reduced by $25,000. This exemption is phased out with higher amounts of income.

Active participation in an activity is also defined.

The $25,000 allowance has not been adjusted for inflation since it was set in 1986.

Passive losses that are disallowed can be carried forward to offset future passive income.

Needless to say, this is another complicated patch that was made to the tax law to solve the perceived problem of taxpayers using rental activities that generate losses to offset and reduce total taxable income.

With the change proposed above to allow only straight-line depreciation, the likelihood of losses in real estate activity is reduced.

Eliminating this provision of requiring passive activity losses to be used only against passive activity income would greatly reduce the complexity of the income tax law in this area.

Since the purpose of the income tax law should not be to direct taxpayers as to what activity they can engage in. Also, since the goal of tax reform is to simplify the whole income tax process, this provision is high on the list of provisions that should be reversed and eliminated.

27. Eliminate tax-free trades of like-kind property.

If a taxpayer sells one property and within the allowed time frame buys a like-kind property or if the taxpayer exchanges the first property directly for a different like-kind property, the tax law allows the taxpayer to not report a gain on the disposal of the first property. That gain is deferred by reducing the tax basis of the second property by the amount of gain that was deferred and not recognized.

The idea, perhaps, behind this concept is that no economic gain was received but only that the taxpayer shifted from one property to another. Of course, in inventing this concept, the income tax law ushered in all kinds of techniques to establish the tax-free exchange. This has fed an industry of tax-free exchange professionals. In addition, there have been occasions when an exchange was arranged but not well considered. The property that replaced the first property was acquired without proper review and worked out to be a poor economic decision.

In addition, the question might be raised as to why this maneuver is allowed for like kinds of real estate but not for other types of property, including stocks and bonds.

In pursuit of income tax simplification, this is another provision that has been around for 38 years, and it is time to put it under our tax simplification microscope and eliminate it from the law.

28. Time to update the rules on selling your personal residence

The rules about selling your home and paying a tax on the gain were changed in 1997. At that time there was an exclusion allowed amounting to $125,000.

President Clinton signed the Taxpayer Relief Act, which allowed taxpayers to exclude the first $250,000 of gain on the sale of a primary residence from taxable income ($500,000 for married couples filing jointly).

Any gain over the exclusion amount is taxed as a capital gain, and any losses are not deductible.

The exclusion amounts of $250,000 and $500,000 are not and have not been adjusted for inflation. That's one thing that needs to be changed. Also, why is a single person given an exclusion much lower than a married taxpayer?

If the exclusion had been adjusted for inflation since 1997, the $500,000 would have grown to $974,000. This is an example where our "income tax" law is more than a tax on income. It's also a tax on inflation. Same house, same cost, but the price has increased as a result of inflation. The seller cannot go out and buy some other major ticket item with the proceeds after income tax and get a comparable price on the purchase. That taxpayer gets no inflation discount when they reuse or reinvest the proceeds.

As my boss once said, "don't assume the income tax rules are fair." He is proven right again. Let's fix that non-income tax law. And while we are at it, let's change the rules and use one exclusion amount, whether the taxpayer is married or single.

29. Provide a new service to taxpayers to reduce their costs, anxiety, and fees to their accountants.

Each taxpayer is required to pay a portion of their taxes over the course of the tax year rather than at the date the tax return is filed. For example, if a taxpayer incurs an income tax of $20,000 for the year 2025, they must have paid at least 90% of the $20,000, generally in equal quarterly installments, by the last installment date, which would be 1/15/2026. If the taxpayer in this example has $6,000 income tax withholding paid through their employment, the taxpayer needs to pay $12,000 in estimated taxes in quarterly installments of $3,000.

The penalty rate for 2024 went into effect near the end of 2023. It is the highest penalty rate since 2007. The IRS sets the penalty rate every quarter. The taxpayer uses form 1040 ES to calculate the amount of estimated taxes to pay for the year. In addition, the taxpayer uses form 2210 to calculate the amount of underpayment penalty due with each year's return.

Why don't we create a service to help the taxpayers to avoid this worry and cost. The filing of these forms and the assessing of the penalty can largely be avoided by creating a new IRS deposit account. In this manner, the taxpayer can put money on deposit with the IRS. At the end of the year, and when the tax return is filed, the taxpayer can elect to apply some portion of the balance in the IRS deposit account to the payment of the tax due. With enough funds in the deposit account, the taxpayer can avoid any underpayment penalty.

Each year, the taxpayer will get an accounting for their IRS deposit account. Any balance not used by the payment of estimated taxes will be credited with an interest amount based on the one-year borrowing rate that the U. S. Treasury incurs for its one-year maturities of U.S. Treasury bills.

This will give the taxpayer assurance that they won't be paying the penalty. It will give them a fair rate of return on their funds. It will also give the U.S. Treasury a source for borrowing by establishing these deposit accounts.

30. All of the thresholds and brackets should be adjusted annually for inflation.

This seems to be a "no-brainer," and yet the income tax law is loaded with inconsistencies regarding threshold levels, base amounts, tax brackets, etc. Some get annual adjustments to reflect inflation. Some don't. There is no apparent reason for this other than maybe it wasn't considered in the cases where no inflation adjustment was provided.

One of the best examples of a fixed limit that hasn't been changed is the limit on net capital losses that can be deducted in any one year. This limit has been in place since 1978. If the initial amount of $3,000 had been adjusted for the change in the CPI -U index each year, the capital loss limit would now be $14,000.

There are several other amounts that are written into the income tax law that don't get adjusted for inflation. However, some do. It's time to make that adjustment an automatic factor in income tax law.

In the example of the limit on the net capital loss deduction above, if $3,000 was determined to be a reasonable limit in 1978, would it be less reasonable after inflation of 366%? This may be an example where inflation is the friend of the IRS.

31. Let's put all of the tax laws in their own Lock Box

Make it "ironclad' as Al Gore suggested he would do with the Social Security fund years ago.

All future modifications to the income tax code will be limited to changes in the tax rates and changes in allowed bonus depreciation. Tax rates will not be able to be raised from the initial tax rate table. This will create a stable income tax system not continually changing with shifts of political majorities.

Any other changes to the income tax law shall require a 2/3's majority vote by both the Senate and the House of Representatives.

Leaving open the ability to change tax rates and to make changes in bonus depreciation for capital equipment additions each year, will give Congress two powerful methods to affect the economic growth of the nation. But limiting the levers to only these two will make these occasional changes totally transparent and end the practice of inserting a multitude of social policies each year in the tax law.

32. Otherwise, what could happen is the whole new start of another tax monster.

The current law has grown and grown over its 110 years of existence. We can't let that happen again.

On March 19, 2024, Senator Elizabeth Warren issued a press release to reintroduce her "Ultra-Millionaire Tax" on fortunes over $50 Million. She called it the "Ultra-Millionaire Tax Act." Her press release called it "popular, comprehensive legislation that would bring in at least $3 Trillion over ten years.

She would give birth to another way to tax people by assessing a tax each year of 2% for every dollar of net worth over $50 Million. Assume a taxpayer averages a net return of 8% on all assets, including personal property, homes, and farms; this would be an additional tax of 25% on that income. It would increase the taxpayers' federal tax rate to 65.7%. That's bad in itself.

Even worse, it creates a whole new set of tax laws, tax forms, tax provisions, tax maneuvering, tax advisers, and tax examiners.

If the senator wants to increase taxes, here's a suggestion: increase the tax rates. If 40.7% on everything over $609,000 isn't enough, raise the rate from 40.7% to whatever is enough. You don't have to add all this complication to a very complicated income tax law.

This is an example of why a new income tax law has to severely restrict changes that are made by the legislators for every situation or new idea they conceive.

Let's try to keep it simple and consistent. We must put something in the law that keeps the lawmakers disciplined and focused.

Senator Warren's press release proudly noted that her proposed legislation is co-sponsored by about 40 other legislators and endorsed by more than 30 unions, political committees, and lobbying organizations.

The interesting common denominator about all of those co-sponsors and endorsers is that none of them would pay one more penny of tax if the legislation were passed. They would also not have to incur the cost of complying with the new tax. Tax laws are so easy to pass if they don't affect the supporters of the legislators who dream up the new taxes.

If they want to get creative, they need to think about controlling federal expenditures and not how to create new tax systems and higher taxes.

33. Address that Huge Elephant that is shaking the whole room but no one addresses - the pending insolvency of the Social Security and Medicare system.

Everyone knows this problem exists. Everyone knows it's the biggest problem facing the Federal government's financial future. No one wants to bring it up and fix it.

Wrapping up the solution to this major issue with Social Security and Medicare at the same time that the income tax law is reformed and simplified is the perfect time to notice the huge elephant in the room and get it under control. The new income tax system will be adjusted to provide a long-term solution to the nation's rapidly increasing national debt. Changes to the Social Security and Medicare revenues and expenditures will put that system on a solid financial trajectory as well.

As noted above, "Make No Small Plans."

34. Provide a look back on the tax calculation in the first year of the new tax law being put into place.

There should be a failsafe in the tax law for the first year of implementation. This will go hand in hand with the one exception allowing legislators the authority to make changes to the tax law in the first year to change the results of inequitable unintended circumstances.

The new law should allow any taxpayer with taxable income less than $100,000 in the first year to elect to use the taxpayer's prior year tax as the tax for the first year of implementation of the income tax reform laws. This can only apply to a taxpayer who filed as a single taxpayer in the prior year and is unmarried in the first year. It would also apply to taxpayers who filed jointly in the prior year and are married in the second year.

35. Oh, by the way, and then there is the National Debt

The United States currently has a national debt totaling $33 Trillion. The interest due on that amount of debt is $875 Billion. One problem with the debt and the interest due is that they are so large it's hard to grasp the size of what is owed and the amount of interest that has to be paid.

As the debt goes up, so does the interest being paid go up. As interest rates go up, so does the amount of interest due on the debt go up.

The Council on Foreign Relations wrote an article on "The U. S. National Debt Dilemma" dated December 23, 2023. In the article, they gave a breakdown of the 2022 U. S. Budget as follows:

	$Billions	Percent of Total
Net interest payments (lower rates back then)	$ 475	8%
Education, transportation, housing, veterans, other	$ 751	12%
Defense	$ 910	14%
Some veteran's benefits, federal retirement	$ 520	8%
Student loans	$ 482	8%
Income security programs	$ 581	9%
Medicaid	$ 592	9%
Medicare	$ 747	12%
Social Security	$1200	19%

As annual budget deficits continue, the total national debt increases. Same with interest rates. As they go up, the total interest due goes up. For example, the 2023 deficit was $1.7 Trillion. The interest paid for 2023 was $875 Billion. Creating a simple worksheet based on continuing deficits and varying interest rates, it's not hard to predict that the interest expense portion of the Federal budget could reach $2.5 Trillion in the next 20 years.

That would be double the 2022 budget for Social Security, which itself is on the path to insolvency.

Does anyone in Washington see flashing red lights here?

Putting brakes on federal spending is one way to address this dangerous trend. Unfortunately, a big part of the budget consists of interest, defense, and non-discretionary spending. It's highly unlikely that the budget can be cut to any significant degree.

That leaves the need for higher tax revenues. If the nation is going to control its destiny by controlling its debt and funding its Medicare and Social Security obligations, it must increase its tax revenues. This can be done by greatly simplifying the tax system. It can be done by eliminating the use of income tax laws to fund all manner of additional programs. It can be done by eliminating deductions and tax exemptions for various "special" types of income. And it can be done by reducing the income tax system to a simplified formula of income and straight forward and uniform income tax rates. It really is time to take the medicine, and the medicine is not so bad that it can't be taken now, but not much later.

If you picture the United States Treasury as a big freight train running downhill from the Rocky Mountains to the Pacific Ocean. If you consider that there are no engineers running the Locomotive. If you think of all of the freight cars behind, filled with all of the baked-in expenses of the government – Medicare, Social Security, Education, Defense, Veterans Benefits, a very long train of cars pushing forward. Then think of the fuel, which in this illustration would be the increasing interest expense on the Federal debt, feeding the train's engines has been tipped forward and is flowing faster and faster into the chambers, feeding this train further and faster. It's just a question of when it crashes and where.

36. Who is going to bring this book across the Swamp and get a fresh start for our income tax laws?

We need the leadership and clear focus of our founding president and we need the call to our better angels as spoken by our great president, Abraham Lincoln.

This will not be an easy task, but it will be a game changer for a lot of our problems, especially those of a fiscal nature.

We have built a monstrosity of a tax system. We have, at the same time, built a mountain of debt, a mountain that grows with each yearly deficit. We have made promises to all of our citizens that they will have a solvent Social Security and Medicare system.

With the elections of 2024 in front of us, now is the time to call for this new plan and a plan that can right the ship.

When you have read this book, ask your representatives and candidates whether they will work for a solvent government and whether they will clean up all of the financial problems in the Swamp. Our representatives need to change years of mismanagement and rotten thinking. Clean up the system. It really is the time to step forward and change the government so that the government truly is, as Lincoln promised, "of the people, by the people, for the people… and shall not perish."

37. Corporations

Unfortunately, this book proposing major tax reform for our income tax system was written under a deadline to be published so as to be considered during congressional and presidential deliberations and elections in 2024.

Swinging an ax or sledgehammer through pages and pages of tax law and trying to reduce the law to a simpler version of its current ponderous self is a tall and tiring task.

To meet the self-imposed deadline, a detailed review of corporate tax law is not possible.

However, it seems that the 2017 TCJA reduction of the corporate tax rate was far too big, taking the tax rate for corporations down from 35% to 21%. That's a 40% reduction in rate.

In the proposed changes in individuals' rates discussed above, the top rate is proposed to be 41% for the highest income bracket. The new rate is also set so as to eliminate the 3.8% special tax on net investment income. That seems to be a much fairer rate for corporations to pay and compares well to the top individual rate. At a minimum, the corporate rate should be set back to the 35% level before the TCJA cut. This restitution of the original rate will raise significant revenue for the Federal government, which can be used to reduce the annual deficits, the national debt, and the impending Social Security and Medicare fund crisis.

Cutting the corporate rate was a very generous gift to the corporate taxpayers. It's time to go back to reality.

Other corporate income law changes that should be considered are:

1. Eliminate the alternative minimum income tax.
2. Eliminate the Financial statement income as an alternative income to tax.
3. No more tax-free municipal bond income for corporations or individuals
4. Expense research and development costs as incurred.
5. Eliminate limits on corporate interest expense deductions.
6. Use the much simpler depreciation calculations discussed above for individuals.
7. Adopt the First In First Out method as the only allowable method of costing out inventory.
8. Eliminate depletion deductions on mining and fossil fuel production.

There are many long-established laws governing corporation income taxes. The many aspects of corporate business operations are more complicated than what an individual must confront and incur.   Thus, it seems prudent to keep the many historically determined methods of corporate taxation. At another time, and with more time to do, simplification reviews can be performed for the corporations, LLCs, S corporations, and partnerships.

38. Estate and Gift Taxes

The TCJA provided for a $10,000,000 exclusion amount for estate and gift taxes. This exclusion is adjusted annually for inflation and is currently $13,610,000. Estates higher than that amount are assessed an estate tax of 40% on the excess. Yes, I did say 40%, a BIG slice of the pie.

If that provision is allowed to expire, the exclusion will be dropped to $5,000,000, adjusted annually for inflation.

For those subject to the estate tax, it is very motivating to do estate tax planning to reduce that high cost as much as possible. There are a host of maneuvers that are entered into to try to retain the assets of a taxpayer. Some are successful and achieve the objectives of the taxpayer. Some create other problems and prove not to be the best economic outcome for the taxpayer or the country.

In the above discussion of the income tax, we have noted the much higher taxes that are paid by the higher income earners. The estate tax, at the end, takes a very big last helping of that taxpayer's net worth.

Here is where we should take the advice of Senator Warren. She has identified the $50,000,000 hurdle at which she would like to create a new wealth tax to be paid annually by those with over that amount of wealth.

Taking into account the target that has been carried on their backs by those taxpayers all of their lives, I suggest that the estate and gift tax exclusion be set at Senator Warren's suggested amount of $50,000,000 and that it be adjusted annually for inflation.

Here is a little fairness for the higher-income taxpayer: Give them a break at the end of their tax-paying life.

39. Conclusion

The overall result of these changes will be designed to give an increase in income to low income taxpayers and to free these citizens from income tax; to put Social Security and Medicare on a sustainable footing; to increase the effective tax rates for taxpayers earning more than $400,000; to increase the corporate tax rates from 21% to 35%; to provide a tax system that is competitive with other countries; to provide a net increase in federal tax revenues to reduce the federal debt to be equal to some reasonable percentage of GDP; and **to greatly simplify the income tax (and various other special costs and benefits) system, known as "our (crazy) income tax law" The** premise of this book is that the Income tax system is broken and it has to be fixed.

As you see as you read through all of these pages, the book proposes a massive reduction in the rules and laws which combined are called our "income tax" law. That in itself is bold face lie. This is not an income law, it is a bunch of words grafted and created and amended and perverted over the 110 years since the 16th Amendment to the Constitution was adopted. It is not an income tax law in the sense it asks the taxpayer to determine their income and then pay a percentage of that income to the government. It is actually a bunch of laws interspersed like a Christmas tree, full of this and that from fruits and nuts to green energy and fossil fuel, to rules on employee parking and rules on performing artists' expenses and teachers' $300 expense allowance. On top of that, if you make a mistake in calculating your tax, or takes you too long to figure it out –Ba-boom down comes the big IRS penalty; only money if you are lucky. Jail time if you are not. There is a concept in criminal law coined as "entrapment." The tax laws are a big set of entrapment mechanisms. Let the taxpayer beware.

The Congressional Budget Office can do the number crunching. Looking at it from an overview of 40,000 feet, the lower income taxpayers will receive a benefit, and have more money in their pockets.

The higher income taxpayers and corporations will be paying more taxes.

In the past, I would have said that higher taxes will have a bad effect on the economy, resulting in less growth, fewer jobs, less investment.

Here's the difference. These higher taxes will not go to more government spending. These taxes will go to getting our hands around the government debt, and the unfunded liabilities of Social Security and Medicare, and to provide income to the citizens with a lower income

These higher taxes will insure the solvency of the United States.

That is the best prescription for a healthy economy. These higher taxes will be a boost to the economy.

If this appears to be a hatchet job, when one sees a big amount of the 2,448 pages of tax law scattered on and covering the floor, after implementing the recommendations in this book, to that observation, I say this. Look at the small neatly bound set of pages that are sitting on the desk after everything is boiled down to simply an income tax law.

What we will have is a simpler to understand set of instructions for the taxpayer to follow. We will have much fewer hours spent on preparing returns and auditing returns. We will have built another wall, this one built to protect the simplicity and consistency of how we are taxed. This alone will pay great dividends in being able to plan, whether it be personal planning to determine how to reach your financial goals, or whether it be a large corporation thankful that the unknown unknowns popping up almost annually with changes in the tax law, can now be put in a vault and never let out again.

Simplification will also be a blessing to those in the Congressional Budget Office who are called upon to project the revenues and expenses of the Federal government. Ask any statistician/accountant/economist: In which situation would you be more comfortable creating a computer model to project the Federal government budget:

1. In the current world where there are tax credits, several tax brackets, tax breaks with thresholds that eliminate tax breaks, multiple capital gain tax rates, exemptions and exclusions, multiple social policy considerations, complicated rules to determine which complicated laws apply to a given taxpayer, or

2. A new scenario where there is one set of tax brackets, no tax credits, and limits on how the tax laws can be manipulated in the future.

If those individuals are thinking about being more accurate and confident of their results, they would vote for number 2. If they are concerned about their being needed to make these calculations and employed in that less than rewarding endeavor for the rest of their career, they would vote for number 1.

Taxpayers, how do you vote?

Here are the basics of the proposed new tax laws:

1. Report your income, with no exclusions except for social security benefits and no deductions except for charitable contributions and a much larger standard deduction.
2. Reference that income calculation to one simple tax table of eight possible tax rates. That's your tax.
3. Subtract what you paid during the year. That's your refund or your tax due.

A similar simplification would take place at the corporate and business level.

What will Congress be allowed to do to change the law in the future? They can change the tax rates down but not up from the proposed law. They can change the bonus depreciation allowances. This gives Congress the ability to raise needed revenue or to stimulate the economy with lower rates or more bonus depreciation. Any other change will require a 2/3's vote of approval by both house of Congress. That provision will put a major lid on future growth of the number of pages in the tax law.

The 2/3's majority vote will be waived during the first year after the tax reform legislation is passed for any changes that need be made to correct errors or significant unintended consequences. The integrity of those changes should be carefully restricted and not allowed to slip from the overall goals of the reform legislation.

We do have artificial intelligence now. Maybe AI can start to figure out the current tax law. I prefer not to have to go that route but to use AI to help the Congressional Budget Office project the cost of future laws ether income tax laws or other laws. With all of the data we accumulate on the components of the tax returns that are filed, we can literally push a button and determine the effect of changes in the tax rates or depreciation.

Another benefit of simplifying the tax law down to a manageable number of pages is that it would greatly simplify all the processing that the IRS has to complete as the millions of tax returns are received. The IRS's computer systems are as patched together and dysfunctional as the "tax law system" which it administers.

On February 15, 2023, the Government Accountability Office (GAO) issued the following report on the state of the IRS IT systems:

"How long does it take to get a payment from the government? Tax refunds, Social Security, Medicare, and Medicaid claims, and much more are processed through Federal IT systems. But many of these systems are decades old AND outdated—which can slow down Federal payments and services and make taxpayer information vulnerable to cyber attacks.

"Congress has long recognized aging IT systems as a costly vulnerability for the Federal government and has appropriated funding to update systems. But many of these efforts face delays and setbacks.

"The IRS uses hundreds of applications, software, and hardware systems that are outdated—25 years or older or written in a programming language that is no longer used. Among these, one example stands out: the primary system that IRS uses to process individual taxpayer account data.

"This critical system helps the IRS assess taxes, generate refunds, update accounts, and more. It was built in the late 1960s, around the same time NASA's Apollo missions were first sending astronauts to the moon. The system has been updated over the years, but maintaining it is getting harder because it relies on a computer programming language (COBOL) that fewer and fewer programmers know.

"Our new report found that the IRS has spent hundreds of millions of dollars trying to update this system. But IRS officials said the system wouldn't be fully replaced until 2030 at the earliest—at which time it will be 60 years old.

"In the report, we recommended establishing time frames for addressing this and other IT modernization needs that affect taxpayers. We also recommended developing a plan that would improve the effectiveness of IRS's efforts."

If the ideas in this book were adopted, the tax law would be simplified for the taxpayers. In addition, it would be greatly simplified for the IRS. Let's target a reduction of 90% of the current tax law when it is rebuilt in its entirety. That means all the computers and all of the programming has to be able to contend with only 10% of the current variables and calculations. This simplification works both ways. That 2030 date projection might actually be met and even be beat. Plus, it would change the IRS effectiveness across the board. Just think of the day when you call the IRS, get a human voice answering, and a person that can find your account and give you an answer on the first phone call.

To borrow the thoughts of a great church hymn "What a Day that Will Be:"

There is coming a day,
When no heart aches shall come,
No more clouds in the sky,
No more tears to dim the eye,
All is clarity forever more,
On that happy golden shore,
What a day, glorious day that will be.

What a day that will be,
When the tax law I shall see,
And all the tax laws I embrace,
The Congress who saved me by their grace;
When the IRS takes me by the hand,
And leads me to the tax deadline Promised Land,
What a day, glorious day that will be.

There'll be no sorrow there,
No more complex burdens do I bear,
No more confusion, no more pain,
No more teeth gnashing over there;
And forever I will be,
With the Congress who saved me,
What a day, glorious day that will be.

What a day that will be,
When my completed return I shall see,
And I look upon that page.
The change that saved me from such rage;
What a day, glorious day that will be.

Perhaps, this conclusion should have been provided at the beginning of this book, but at the end of the book, it gives one last call for a complete rebuild of the income tax system.

With the changes discussed above, the goal will be to provide more economic benefits to those on the lower end of the economic ladder. It will ask for more taxes from the higher income taxpayers, but in exchange it will promise consistency and the ability to plan into the future with a fixed set of rules, no more moving the goal posts. It will provide a path to solvency for Social Security and Medicare and for the Federal debt. Hopefully, it will provide focus and knowledge to Congress as future federal programs are added or changed. The management of the Federal budget will be done within the context of what is and what is not fiscally responsible.

This will be a "page burner," and a "game changer" for America.

Finally, and in conclusion, this is a call to America and to our Congress. We need to take a hold of our tax system, our promises for health care and retirement, and our national debt. This book recommends some big ideas. The big ideas are all meant to work as a solution to a set of problems that the Congress knows is out there. They just can't get their hands around it. They are boxed in by party politics and big political contributions.

40. The Secret Formula for the Federal Government

After all of the preceding words of explanation and history about our crazy income tax system: Here is the biggest, most obvious, and totally logical REVEAL of all.

Fixing our income taxes and national debt and Social Security and Medicare unfunded liabilities is simple math: Compute the following:

A. Start with the total of all taxable income in the United States

Subtract the taxable income of all taxpayers earning less than $100,000.

This is the available income to be taxed.

B. Compare that to the total of the following items:

The net annual budgeted expenditures for the operation of the Federal government.

The targeted annual reduction of the national debt and unfunded Social Security and Medicare liabilities.

The total of refunds made to taxpayers with negative taxable income.

This total is what has to be collected.

If A is $30 Trillion and B is $12 Trillion, then the average income tax rate as a percentage of taxable income should be 40%.

Spread this average tax rate to all individual taxpayers from $100,000 of adjusted gross income on up, and to all corporate and business entities.

There should be no disconnect between government expenditures and tax rates. The one should determine the other, all of the other stuff in the way of this calculation is what makes solving our fiscal crisis so difficult.

This ratio is so important, so logical and so simple, that it is probably not a new ratio in the study of governmental solvency.

However, I have never personally read about it and noted that it is considered in any review of new legislation or changes in government finances.

Therefore, as Roald Amundsen was the first person to plant a flag on the South Pole, I am taking no chances that my discovery of this ratio should ever be dismissed. I hereby name the ratio as the JC Ratio.

The JC Ratio needs to be calculated often and monitored continuously. When the ratio goes above 40, it is my opinion that the government is teetering close to insolvency. As the ratio goes above 40, taxpayers will begin moving their income to tax friendlier countries. With each such move, the ratio will move higher.

If and when the ratio does reach 40, the government must study the components of the ratio, and reduce spending commitments, reduce funding plans to reduce the government debt and unfunded future liabilities, or create more taxable income.

Each change in the tax system, or government spending should be made with a recalculation of the JC ratio.

The JC Ratio will be used to cause the government to focus on the financial effects of the laws passed by Congress and the President.

These things can no longer be done in a vacuum without a determination of the effect on the Federal balance sheet. This is no different than an American family deciding to buy a new car, obtain a new car loan and allocate some of their cash flow to the repayment of the loan. Will their cash flow carry the new loan?

Will the government's new programs be compatible with the longer term goal of meeting the government's legal obligations?

41. Short memorandum to Congress

To: Congress

From: We the American People

Subject: Pending insolvency of Medicare, Social Security and U. S. government

This is the time to get us and you out of the box and get your hands around our critical fiscal problems. It is NOW time for solutions. The best thing you can do is be straightforward and keep it simple. Don't waste time and don't wait until the deadline. Let's get it fixed!

42: Tickets to IRS tax code burning party

Ticket to the IRS Page Burning Event in Washington, DC, in front of the IRS building.

The date and time to be determined based on the passage of a Federal Reform the Income Tax Act, which will free taxpayers from hours of tax return preparation and expenses related to professional tax advisers.

Recommend an early arrival. Parking will not be available close to the event.

Ticket to the IRS Page Burning Event in Washington, DC, in front of the IRS building.

Date and time to be determined based on the passage of a Federal Reform the Income Tax Act, which will free taxpayers from hours of tax return preparation and expenses related to professional tax advisers.

Recommend an early arrival. Parking will not be available close to the event.

References

(1) Who pays and doesn't pay federal income? Taxes in the U. S.? Pew Research Center, By Dew DeSilver: April 18, 2023; page 8.

(2) Federal Income Tax Problems – 1922; Dodd, Mead, and Company; E. E. Rossmoor; page iii.

(3) Transcript of written testimony before the U. S. Senate Committee on Finance on November 9, 2023; William McBride, Vice president of Federal Tax Policy, Tax Foundation; page 16.

(4) We all want simpler taxes. Here's why that's so complicated; The Wall Street Journal; by Laura Sauders; page1.

(5) Statistica

(6) Quote Investigator, November 2010

(7) Teachdemocracy.org website, "The Income Tax Amendment: Most Thought It Was a Great Idea in 1913."

(8) The Brookings Institute, "How Did the TCJA Affect Incentives for Charitable Giving?", 2022.

(9) Tax Foundation, "Latest Data Shows that the Tax Cuts and Jobs Act Did Not Dampen Charitable Giving<" June 22, 2020.

Appendix A: "Expiring Provisions in the Tax Cuts and Jobs Act," Congressional Research Services

Reference Table: Expiring Provisions in the "Tax Cuts and Jobs Act" (TCJA, P.L. 115-97)

November 21, 2023

Congressional Research Service

https://crsreports.congress.gov

R47846

Contents

Tables

Contacts

A variety of temporary changes enacted as part of P.L. 115-97, commonly referred to as the Tax Cuts and Jobs Act (TCJA), are scheduled to expire. Many of these provisions affect individuals and families and are scheduled to expire at the end of 2025. Others affecting businesses, including pass-through businesses, are scheduled to expire between 2025 and 2028.

As Congress considers whether and to what extent to extend these temporary TCJA provisions, **Table 1** provides for each provision:

- a brief overview and how it will change upon the scheduled expiration of the TCJA;
- the budgetary score, both at enactment and if extended permanently
  - a **negative number (-)** generally indicates reduced revenues and hence an **increase in the deficit**,
  - a **positive number (+)** generally indicates increased revenues and hence a **reduction in the deficit**;
- the relevant section of the TCJA;
- the amended section of the Internal Revenue Code (IRC); and
- the expiration date.

Budgetary Cost

At the time of the law's passage, the Joint Committee on Taxation (JCT) estimated that the TCJA would cost $1.5 trillion between FY2018 and FY2027.[1] The Congressional Budget Office (CBO) and JCT have estimated that extensions of all provisions that are scheduled to either expire or become less generous would cost $3.5 trillion between FY2023 and FY2033, although most of these effects would begin in FY2026. More detailed estimates of the provisions' budgetary effects can be found in CBO's supplemental data.[2]

Delayed Onset Provisions

In addition to these expiring provisions, several TCJA provisions featured *delayed onsets* that are expected to make certain tax benefits related to business—including those related to the R&D expenditures—less generous and hence raise revenue. Congress may consider modifying those as well. For more information on these provisions, see "Delayed Onset Tax Provisions in the TCJA" on page 16.

Other Resources

For an overview of all the provisions enacted by the TCJA, including permanent provisions which are not included below, see CRS Report R45092, *The 2017 Tax Revision (P.L. 115-97): Comparison to 2017 Tax Law*. Other temporary tax provisions that were not enacted by the TCJA—and which are commonly referred to as "tax extenders"—are also scheduled to expire at the end of 2025. Consequently, their expiration coincides with the expiration of most of the TCJA's changes to individual income tax provisions. More information on those non-TCJA expiring provisions can be found in CRS Report R47252, *Expired and Expiring Temporary Tax*

---

[1] Joint Committee on Taxation, *Estimated Budget Effects of The Conference Agreement for H.R.1, The Tax Cuts and Jobs Act*, December 18, 2017, JCX-67-17.

[2] Congressional Budget Office, *Budgetary Outcomes Under Alternative Assumptions About Spending and Revenues*, Supplemental Data, May 2023, https://www.cbo.gov/publication/59154#data.

Provision	TCJA	Scheduled Expiration of TCJA
permanently: +$0.1 billion (FY2024-FY2033).		
Itemized deduction for miscellaneous expenses *JCT budgetary cost estimate of TCJA changes at enactment and CBO budgetary cost estimate if TCJA changes extended permanently: Included in combined cost estimates of all changes to itemized deductions (above).*	There is no itemized deduction for certain miscellaneous expenses such as unreimbursed employee expenses or tax preparation fees. *Section 11045 of P.L. 115-97* *IRC Section 67(g)* Expires 12/31/2025	Individual taxpayers who itemize their deductions will be able to deduct miscellaneous expenses to the extent that such expenses collectively exceed 2% of their AGI. Expenses subject to the 2% floor will include unreimbursed employee expenses, tax preparation fees, and certain other expenses. *IRC Sections 62, 67, and 212*
Overall limitation on itemized deductions *JCT budgetary cost estimate of TCJA changes at enactment and CBO budgetary cost estimate if TCJA changes extended permanently: Included in combined cost estimates of all changes to itemized deductions (above).*	The total amount of itemized deductions that can be claimed by a taxpayer is the sum of all allowable itemized deductions and there is no overall limitation on itemized deductions. *Section 11046 of P.L. 115-97* *IRC Section 68(f)* Expires 12/31/2025	For taxpayers with AGI above certain thresholds, the total amount of itemized deductions will be reduced by 3% of the amount by which their AGI exceeds the threshold. (For 2018, before the TCJA, the thresholds once adjusted for inflation would have been $320,000 for married taxpayers filing jointly and $267,700 for singles.) The total reduction will be capped at 80% of the deductions. Itemized deductions not subject to the limitation include deductions for medical and dental expenses, investment interest, charitable contributions, casualty and theft losses, and wagering losses. *IRC Section 68*

Provision	TCJA	Scheduled Expiration of TCJA

Exclusions[a]

Provision	TCJA	Scheduled Expiration of TCJA
Bicycle commuter reimbursement *JCT budgetary cost estimate of TCJA changes at enactment: revenue increase of less than $50 million (FY2018-FY2027).* *CBO budgetary cost estimate if TCJA changes extended permanently: +$136 million (FY2024-FY2033).*	Employer reimbursements for bicycle commuting expenses are considered wage income and therefore subject to income and employment (i.e., "payroll") taxes. *Section 11047 of P.L. 115-97* *IRC Section 132(f)* Expires 12/31/2025	Up to $20 per month of qualified employer reimbursements for bicycle commuting expenses will be excludible from wage income, and hence not subject to either income or employment (i.e., "payroll") taxes. *IRC Section 132(f)*
Moving reimbursement exclusion *JCT budgetary cost estimate of TCJA changes at enactment: +$4.8 billion (FY2018-FY2027).* *CBO budgetary cost estimate if TCJA changes extended permanently: +$6.7 billion (FY2024-FY2033).*	Employer reimbursements for moving expenses are only excludible from income and wages for members of the Armed Forces and pursuant to a military order for a permanent change of station. For all other employees, such benefits are considered wage income and hence subject to income and employment (i.e., "payroll") taxes. *Section 11048 of P.L. 115-97* *IRC Section 132(g)(2)* Expires 12/31/2025	Qualified moving expense reimbursements from an employer will be excludible from an employee's wage income, and hence not subject to either income or employment (i.e., "payroll") taxes. *IRC Section 132*
Combat zone tax benefits for members of the Armed Forces in the Sinai Peninsula *JCT budgetary cost estimate of TCJA changes at enactment: revenue loss of less than $50*	Members of the Armed Forces serving in a combat zone (and their families) are entitled to several tax benefits, including: (1) an exemption from income and employment ("payroll") taxes on certain military pay received during any month in which the member served in a combat zone (IRC Sections 112 and 3401(a)(1)); (2) an exemption from income taxes during the year that the member dies and the year prior while serving in a combat zone (IRC Section 692); (3) special estate tax rules where death occurs in a combat zone (IRC Section 2201);	The Sinai Peninsula will not be statutorily presumed to be a combat zone. Unless the Sinai Peninsula is designated as a combat zone under the usual process (IRC Section 112), members of the Armed Forces serving in this area will not be eligible for combat zone tax benefits. *IRC Sections 2, 112, 692, 2201, 3401, 4253, 6013, and 7508*

Provision	TCJA	Scheduled Expiration of TCJA
million (FY2018-FY2027). *CBO budgetary cost estimate if TCJA changes extended permanently: -$7 million (FY2024-FY2033).*	(4) special benefits to surviving spouses (IRC Sections 2(a)(3) and 6013(f)(1)); (5) an extension of tax deadlines, including for filing returns, making payments, claiming credits or refunds, and certain other deadlines (IRC Section 7508); (6) an exclusion of telephone excise taxes (IRC Section 4253(d)). Typically, combat zones are designated by the President in an Executive Order as an area where the Armed Forces are or have engaged in combat. Under the TCJA, the Sinai Peninsula is statutorily presumed to be a combat zone. *Section 11026 of P.L. 115-97* Expires 12/31/2025	

Alternative Minimum Tax

Provision	TCJA	Scheduled Expiration of TCJA
Alternative minimum tax (AMT) exemption and phaseouts *JCT budgetary cost estimate of TCJA changes: -$637.1 billion (FY2018-FY2027).* *CBO budgetary cost estimate if TCJA changes extended permanently: -$1,088.4 billion (FY2024-FY2033).*	A tax is imposed at 26% on an individual's alternative minimum taxable income, with a higher rate of 28% applied to taxpayers with alternative minimum taxable incomes above $232,600 in 2024. Alternative minimum taxable income (AMTI) starts with taxable income, then adds back certain preference items (such as net operating losses, depreciation, and passive losses all calculated under special AMT rules, state and local taxes, miscellaneous business expenses, and personal exemptions), and then subtracts an AMT exemption amount. (Note: Personal exemptions were effectively eliminated under the TCJA. See "Personal exemptions.") For 2024 the AMT exemption amounts are $85,700 for singles/heads of households and $133,300 for married couples. The AMT exemption amount phases down when a taxpayer's income exceeds a phaseout level. These levels are $578,150 for singles/head of households and $1,156,300 for married couples. These amounts are adjusted for inflation. *Section 12003 of P.L. 115-97* *IRC Section 55* Expires 12/31/2025	The AMT exemption and exemption phaseout will revert to pre-TCJA levels and then both will be adjusted for inflation. For 2018, prior to the TCJA, the higher 28% rate applied to incomes above $191,500 for married couples. For 2018, prior to the TCJA, the exemption amounts were $55,400 for singles/heads of households and $86,200 for married couples and the exemption phaseouts were $123,100 for singles/heads of households and $164,100 for married couples in 2018. (Note: Personal exemptions will again be in effect upon the expiration of the TCJA. See "Personal exemptions.") *IRC Section 55*

Provision	TCJA	Scheduled Expiration of TCJA

ABLE Accounts

Provision	TCJA	Scheduled Expiration of TCJA
Achieving A Better Life Experience (ABLE) account contribution limit *JCT budgetary cost estimate of TCJA changes at enactment: revenue loss of less than $50 million (FY2018-FY2027).* *CBO budgetary cost estimate if TCJA changes extended permanently: -$2 million (FY2024-FY2033).*	ABLE accounts are tax-favored savings accounts intended to encourage qualifying disabled individuals (referred to as "designated beneficiaries") to save money for certain disability-related expenses (in a tax-preferred way) without losing eligibility for certain federal means-tested programs, such as Medicaid. Generally, in a given year an ABLE account cannot receive aggregate contributions in excess of the annual gift tax exemption, which is $18,000 in 2024. Under the TCJA, a designated beneficiary who is employed can contribute an additional amount to their ABLE account (above the annual gift-tax exclusion amount). The additional amount is equal to the lesser of (1) the applicable federal poverty level for a one-person household in the prior year, or (2) the beneficiary's compensation for the year. A beneficiary cannot contribute this additional amount for the year if any contribution is made on their behalf to certain defined contribution plans. *Section 11024(a) of P.L. 115-97* *IRC Section 529A(b)(2)(B)* Expires 12/31/2025	While the gift tax exclusion will still apply, designated beneficiaries will not be able to make the additional contribution of up to the lesser of the federal poverty level for a one-person household or the beneficiary's compensation. *IRC Section 529A*
ABLE accounts and the saver's credit *JCT budgetary cost estimate of TCJA changes at enactment: revenue loss of less than $50 million (FY2018-FY2027).* *CBO budgetary cost estimate if TCJA changes extended permanently: included in the cost of increasing the contribution limit (above)*	Designated beneficiaries who make qualified contributions to their ABLE account can qualify for a nonrefundable saver's credit of up to $1,000. *Section 11024(b) of P.L. 115-97* *IRC Section 25B(d)(1)(D)* Expires 12/31/2025	Designated beneficiaries will not be able to claim the saver's credit for their contributions. Note: the SECURE 2.0 Act of 2022 (Section 103 of P.L. 117-328) included a provision aimed at promoting retirement savings among low-income households that effectively repeals the saver's credit under IRC Section 25B and replaces it with a saver's match under IRC Section 6433, effective 1/1/2027. *IRC Section 25B*

Provision	TCJA	Scheduled Expiration of TCJA
529 to ABLE account rollover *JCT budgetary cost estimate of TCJA changes at enactment: revenue loss of less than $50 million (FY2018-FY2027).* *CBO budgetary cost estimate if TCJA changes extended permanently: -$3 million (FY2024-FY2033).*	Rollovers from a 529 account to an ABLE account (*plus* any other contributions to the account for the year) that are less than or equal to the annual ABLE contribution limit are not subject to income taxation, provided that the accounts have the same designated beneficiary (or the designated beneficiaries of the two accounts are members of the same family). The portion of the rollover (plus any other contributions to the account) in excess of the annual contribution limit is taxable. *Section 11025 of P.L. 115-97* *IRC Section 529(c)(3)(C)(i)(III)* Expires 12/31/2025	All rollovers from 529 accounts to ABLE accounts will be subject to taxation. *IRC Section 529*

Business Provisions

Provision	TCJA	Scheduled Expiration of TCJA
Deduction for pass-through business income—"199A Deduction" *JCT budgetary cost estimate of TCJA changes: -$415 billion (FY2018-FY2027).* *CBO budgetary cost estimate if TCJA changes extended permanently: -$548 billion (FY2024-FY2033).*	Pass-through business income is taxed according to ordinary individual income tax rates. The TCJA created a deduction equal to 20% of qualified business income. The deduction is limited to the greater of 50% of W-2 wages, or 25% of W-2 wages plus 2.5% multiplied by depreciable property (equipment and structures). Specified service trade or businesses (SSTBs)[b] generally may not claim the deduction except in specific circumstances. The deduction limitation and SSTB limitation do not apply if taxable income is less than $191,950 (single) or $383,900 (married) in 2024. These limitations are phased in over a $50,000 (single) and $100,000 (married) range, and thus apply fully if a taxpayer's income is at or above $214,950 (single) and $483,900 (married). *Section 11011 of P.L. 115-97* IRC Section 199A Expires 12/31/2025	The 199A deduction will expire. Hence pass-through business income will generally be taxed according to ordinary individual income tax rates without a deduction for qualified business income.
Limitation on losses for noncorporate taxpayers *JCT budgetary cost estimate of TCJA*	For taxpayers other than C corporations, a deduction in the current year for excess business losses is temporarily disallowed, originally through 2026 by the TCJA and subsequently extended to 2028 by the Inflation Reduction Act (P.L. 117-169, IRA). In addition, such losses are treated as a NOL carryover to the following year.	Businesses will generally be permitted to carry over a net operating loss (NOL) to certain past and future years. Under the passive loss rules, individuals and certain other taxpayers will be limited in their ability to claim deductions and credits from passive trade and business activities, although unused deductions and credits can generally be

Provision	TCJA	Scheduled Expiration of TCJA
changes: +$150 billion (FY2018-FY2027). *CBO budgetary cost estimate if TCJA changes extended permanently: +$137 billion (FY2024-FY2033).*	An excess business loss is the amount that a taxpayer's aggregate deductions attributable to trades and businesses exceed the sum of (1) aggregate gross income or gain attributable to such activities, and (2) $305,000 ($610,000 if married filing jointly) in 2024. For partnerships and S corporations, this provision is applied at the partner or shareholder level. *Section 11012 of P.L. 115-97* *Section 13903 of P.L. 117-169* *IRC Section 461(l)* Expires 12/31/2028	carried forward to the next year. Similarly, certain farm losses may not be deducted in the current year, but can be carried forward to the next year. *IRC Section 461(l)*
Expensing *JCT budgetary cost estimate of TCJA changes: -$86 billion (FY2018-FY2027).* *CBO budgetary cost estimate if TCJA changes extended permanently: -$325 billion (FY2024-FY2033).*	A taxpayer generally must capitalize the cost of property used in a trade or business or held for the production of income and recover such cost over time through annual deductions for depreciation or amortization. The TCJA temporarily allowed full expensing (i.e., 100% bonus depreciation) through 2022, before phasing down ratably through the end of 2026. For long-production-period property, the phasedown period begins after 2024. *Section 13201 of P.L. 115-97* *IRC Section 168(k)* Expires 12/31/2026 (Excluding long production property)	Businesses will generally capitalize the cost of property used in a trade or business or held for the production of income and recover such cost over time through annual deductions for depreciation or amortization without the use of bonus depreciation.
Citrus plants lost by casualty *JCT budgetary cost estimate of TCJA changes: revenue loss of less than $50 million (FY2018-FY2027).* *CBO budgetary cost estimate if TCJA changes extended permanently: -$11 million (FY2024-FY2033).*	The uniform capitalization (UNICAP) rules address the method for determining costs that taxpayers are required to capitalize or treat as inventory. They generally apply to property produced in a trade or business or acquired for resale. One exception is for edible citrus plants lost or damaged by reason of a casualty or similar event. The exception may apply to (A) the taxpayer's cost of replanting such citrus plants, and either (B) costs paid or incurred by other persons if the taxpayer has more than a 50% equity interest in the citrus plants at all times during the year and the other person owns any of the remaining interest and materially participates in the planting or similar activities, or (C) temporarily through the TCJA to third parties if (1) the taxpayer has	The exception for third parties (C) would no longer apply. (The other two exceptions—(A) and (B)—would still apply.) *IRC Section 263A*

Provision	TCJA	Scheduled Expiration of TCJA
	an equity interest of at least 50% in the replanted citrus plants at all times during the year and the other person owns any of the remaining interest, or (2) the other person acquired the taxpayer's entire equity interest in the land on which the citrus plants were located and the replanting is on such land. Section 13207 of P.L. 115-97 IRC Section 263A(d)(2)(C)(ii) Expires 12/22/2027	

Other Provisions

Provision	TCJA	Scheduled Expiration of TCJA
Estate and gift tax *JCT budgetary cost estimate of TCJA changes: -$83.0 billion (FY2018-FY2027).* *CBO budgetary cost estimate if TCJA changes extended permanently: -$126.5 billion (FY2024-FY2033).*	Estate and gift taxes are levied at a rate of 40% on transfers after excluding a fixed amount from taxation. For decedents who die in 2024, the exclusion amount is $13,610,000 per decedent ($10 million per decedent statutorily adjusted annually for inflation). Section 11061 of P.L. 115-97 IRC Section 2010(c)(3)(C) Expires 12/31/2025	The estate and gift tax exclusion amount will be reduced from $10 million per decedent to $5 million per decedent statutorily and then adjusted annually for inflation. IRC Sections 2001 and 2010
Employer credit for paid family and medical leave *JCT budgetary cost estimate of TCJA changes: -$4.3 billion (FY2018-FY2027).* Note that this does not reflect the cost of the subsequent extensions of this provision by P.L. 116-94 and P.L. 116-260. *CBO budgetary cost estimate if TCJA changes extended permanently: -$3.6*	Employers paying wages to employees on family and medical leave may be eligible for a tax credit. The credit amount is calculated as a percentage of wages paid to a qualifying employee while on family and medical leave. If the employers pay 50% of wages normally paid while an employee is on family and medical leave, the credit is 12.5% of wages paid, proportionally increasing to a maximum credit of 25% for paid leave worth 100% of wages normally paid. Employers may claim the credit for up to 12 weeks of paid leave per employee. Leave required by state or local law does not qualify for the credit. Leave provided in excess of legally required minimums may qualify for the credit. For example, if an employer provided a paid family and medical leave benefit with 100% wage replacement, while legally required to provide a 50% wage replacement benefit, the excess 50% may qualify for the credit. However, many state or local laws	No credit will be available for employer-provided paid family and medical leave.

Provision	TCJA	Scheduled Expiration of TCJA
billion (FY2024-FY2033).	regarding paid family or medical leave require a wage replacement rate above 50%, so benefits paid to employees in those jurisdictions are likely not eligible for the credit. As state and local governments continue to adopt paid family and medical leave policies, the pool of employers who are potentially eligible for this credit may be shrinking. Eligible employers are those that allow qualifying full-time employees at least two weeks of paid family and medical leave (with leave time prorated for part-time employees) separate from vacation, personal, or sick leave. A qualifying employee is one who has been employed by the employer for at least one year, and who, during the preceding year, had compensation up to 60% of the compensation threshold for highly compensated employees.[e] *Under TJCA, this credit originally expired on December 31, 2019. The Taxpayer Certainty and Disaster Relief Act of 2019 (Division Q of P.L. 116-94) extended the credit through 2020, while the Taxpayer Certainty and Disaster Tax Relief Act of 2020 (Division EE of P.L. 116-260) extended it through 2025.* *Section 13403 of P.L. 115-97* *Section 142 of Division Q of P.L. 116-94* *Section 119 of Division EE of P.L. 116-260* *IRC Section 45S* Expires 12/31/2025	
Qualified opportunity zones *JCT budgetary cost estimate of TCJA changes: -$1.6 billion (FY2018-FY2027).* *CBO budgetary cost estimate if TCJA changes extended permanently: -$67.3 billion*	Opportunity zones provide several tax benefits to those who invest in these areas, including (1) a temporary deferral of capital gains taxation if gains are reinvested in a qualified opportunity fund; (2) an increase in the investment basis if specific holding periods are met; and (3) a permanent exclusion of the capital gains from income if investments in a qualified opportunity fund are held for at least 10 years (hence, these capital gains are not subject to taxation). No election for deferral of gain is allowed after December 31, 2026. *Section 13823 of P.L. 115-97* *IRC Sections 1400Z-1 and 1400Z-2* Expires 12/31/2026	Investments in opportunity zones will not be eligible for deferral, adjustments to basis, or exclusions on gains.

Sources: CRS analysis of P.L. 115-97 and other laws as noted in the table. IRS Revenue Procedures 17-58 and 23-34.

Notes: This table provides a basic description of the tax provisions in P.L. 115-97. Any deviations from the statutory text are not intended as legal interpretations of such text. The table includes primary citations to the Internal Revenue Code (IRC) for each provision, but other IRC provisions and sources of law may be relevant. Some temporary changes to the TCJA either expired as scheduled before 2025, were repealed, or were made permanent and hence are not included in this table.

a. Forgiven debts are generally considered income and subject to the income tax. Under the TCJA, this provision was modified so student loans discharged due to the death or permanent total disability of the student did not count as gross income through 12/31/2025. Section 9675 of the American Rescue Plan Act (ARPA; P.L. 117-2) modified the TCJA change further so that it applied to virtually any discharged student loan. At the end of 2025, when the ARPA change expires, forgiven student loan debt (including debt forgiven due to death or permanent and total disability) will generally be includible in gross income and hence subject to taxation.

b. An SSTB is a trade or business involving the performance of services in the fields of health, law, accounting, actuarial science, performing arts, consulting, athletics, financial services, investing and investment management, trading or dealing in certain assets, or any trade or business where the principal asset is the reputation or skill of one or more of its employees or owners.

c. For example, according to the most recent information from the IRS, for 2022 the applicable amount of compensation was $135,000. Hence to be a qualifying employee in 2023, the employee could be paid up to $81,000 in 2022.

Delayed Onset Tax Provisions in the TCJA

In addition to the expiring provisions discussed above, the TCJA contained several provisions which have delayed implementation dates. For example, for tax years beginning prior to January 1, 2022, businesses could fully deduct research and experimentation expenses in the year the expenses were incurred. For tax years beginning after December 31, 2021, businesses are required under the TCJA to amortize research and experimentation (R&E) expenses over five years. At the time of consideration, JCT estimated that this provision would generate additional federal revenues of $120 billion (FY2022 through FY2027). Continuing to allow R&E expensing, instead of requiring that such expenditures be amortized, would reduce federal tax revenues by an estimated $153 billion (FY2023-FY2032) according to the Tax Policy Center (TPC).[4]

The TCJA also enacted several business tax provisions—base erosion minimum tax (BEAT), foreign-derived intangible income (FDII), and global intangible low-taxed income (GILTI)—with formulas that will be modified starting in tax years beginning after December 31, 2025, and, for the modified limitation on the deduction for business interest, starting in tax years beginning after December 31, 2021. The effects of these formula changes were not separately estimated at the time of consideration, though all of the modifications would generate additional tax revenue. Delaying the formula changes would reduce federal revenue by $14 billion (FY2024-FY2033) for BEAT and a combined $111 billion (FY2024-FY2033) for FDII and GILTI.[5]

Author Information

Margot L. Crandall-Hollick
Specialist in Public Finance

Brendan McDermott
Analyst in Public Finance

Donald J. Marples
Specialist in Public Finance

---

[4] For more information, see Tax Policy Center, "Model Estimates, T22-0163R - Modify Certain Business Provisions, Make CTC Fully Refundable, and Extend Expansion of EITC for Workers without Qualifying Children, Impact on Tax Revenue, 2023-42 Fiscal Years," https://www.taxpolicycenter.org/model-estimates/modify-business-provisions-and-child-tax-credit-and-earned-income-tax-credit-15.

[5] Congressional Budget Office, *Budgetary Outcomes Under Alternative Assumptions About Spending and Revenues*, Supplemental Data, May 2023, https://www.cbo.gov/publication/59154#data.

Disclaimer

This document was prepared by the Congressional Research Service (CRS). CRS serves as nonpartisan shared staff to congressional committees and Members of Congress. It operates solely at the behest of and under the direction of Congress. Information in a CRS Report should not be relied upon for purposes other than public understanding of information that has been provided by CRS to Members of Congress in connection with CRS's institutional role. CRS Reports, as a work of the United States Government, are not subject to copyright protection in the United States. Any CRS Report may be reproduced and distributed in its entirety without permission from CRS. However, as a CRS Report may include copyrighted images or material from a third party, you may need to obtain the permission of the copyright holder if you wish to copy or otherwise use copyrighted material.

Appendix B: Written Testimony before the U. S. Senate Committee on Finance, titled: "Examining How the Tax Code Affects High-Income Individuals and Tax Planning Strategies," by William McBride and Stephen Entin, The Tax Foundation

Hearing Title: "Examining How the Tax Code Affects High-Income Individuals and Tax Planning Strategies"

November 9, 2023

William McBride

Vice President of Federal Tax Policy and Stephen J. Entin Fellow in Economics, Tax Foundation

The Size and Distribution of the Federal Tax Burden

Chairman Wyden, Ranking Member Crapo, and distinguished members of the Senate Finance Committee, thank you for the opportunity to provide testimony on the distribution of the federal tax burden. I am William McBride, Vice President of Federal Tax Policy and Stephen J. Entin Fellow in Economics at the Tax Foundation, where I focus on how we can improve our federal tax code.

Today, my testimony will focus on four points. First, I will describe the current federal tax system, showing that tax collections in recent years are well above historical averages and the burden is highly progressive. Second, I will describe how the tax code's increasing complexity adds to this burden, raising compliance costs for taxpayers and administrative costs for the Internal Revenue Service (IRS). Third, I will describe the economic costs of the tax code's high marginal income tax rates, which slow economic growth and reduce living standards.

Finally, I will recommend ways to reform the federal tax code to reduce complexity and improve economic incentives, grow the economy, benefit low- and middle-income workers, and raise sufficient revenues at or above current levels.

Recent Federal Tax Collections Are Above Average and Set to Go Higher

As a result of the economic recovery coming out of the pandemic and surging inflation, federal tax collections hit an all-time high of $4.9 trillion in fiscal year (FY) 2022, topping the prior year's record collections by $850 billion.[1] As a share of gross domestic product (GDP), federal tax collections in FY 2022 reached a multi-decade high of about 19.4 percent, up from 17.6 percent in the prior fiscal year and near the last peak of 20.0 percent set during the dot-com bubble in FY 2000.[2]

Only two other years in U.S. history saw federal tax collections as a share of GDP exceed the FY 2022 level, both during World War II: in 1943, federal tax collections reached 20.5 percent of GDP before falling to 19.9 percent in 1944. FY 2022 tax collections exceeded the post-war average of 17.2 percent of GDP by 2.2 percentage points.

In FY 2022, individual income tax collections contributed the most to the surge in federal tax collections, growing 29 percent to $2.6 trillion in FY 2022 from $2.0 trillion in FY 2021. Payroll taxes grew 13 percent to $1.5 trillion in FY 2022 from $1.3 trillion in FY 2021, while corporate taxes grew 14 percent to $425 billion from $372 billion, and other revenues grew 13 percent to $356 billion from $316 billion.

Individual income tax collections reached 10.4 percent of GDP in FY 2022, the highest level on record. That level substantially exceeded the prior record of 9.9 percent of GDP set in FY 2000 as well as the World War II-era record of 9.2 percent of GDP set in FY 1944.[3]

The surge in individual income tax revenue is partly attributable to growth in capital gains revenue due to booming stock and housing markets in 2021, itself a function of inflationary fiscal and monetary stimulus during the pandemic.[4] The Congressional Budget Office (CBO) estimates that capital gains realizations and revenue roughly doubled during the pandemic years: realizations grew to $2.0 trillion in 2021 and $1.7 trillion in 2022 from $881 billion in 2019 while revenues grew to $304 billion in FY 2021 and $378 billion in FY 2022 from $169 billion in FY 2019.[5]

As the inflationary boom of 2021 turned into a bust in 2022, and as the Federal Reserve raised interest rates to fight the inflation, federal tax collections dropped about 9 percent to $4.4 trillion in FY 2023, or about 16.5 percent of GDP.[6] The largest decline was for individual income taxes, which fell $456 billion, or 17 percent, to $2.2 trillion, apparently due in large part to a drop in revenue as the stock and housing markets deflated. CBO's preliminary analysis also points to "higher-than-anticipated claims" of the Employee Retention Credit, a pandemic-era program that spawned a cottage industry until the IRS recently halted

1   William McBride, "Inflation is Surging, So Are Federal Tax Collections," Tax Foundation, Oct. 13, 2022, https://taxfoundation.org/federal-tax-collections-inflation-surging/; Congressional Budget Office, Budget and Economic Data, https://www.cbo.gov/data/budget-economic-data.

2   Because the Bureau of Economic Analysis recently revised GDP up considerably for several recent years including 2022, tax revenue as a share of GDP has come down relative to earlier estimates.

3   Office of Management and Budget, Historical Tables, Table 2.3-Receipts by Source as Percentages of GDP: 1934-2028, https://www.whitehouse.gov/omb/budget/historical-tables/. A similar measure from the Bureau of Economic Analysis (BEA) indicates federal and state individual income taxes as a share of personal income reached an all-time high of 14.4 percent in calendar year 2022. See BEA, National Income and Product Accounts, Table 2.1 Personal Income and its Disposition, https://www.bea.gov/itable/national-gdp-and-personal-income.

4   William McBride, "Inflation is Surging, So Are Federal Tax Collections," Tax Foundation, Oct. 13, 2022, https://taxfoundation.org/federal-tax-collections-inflation-surging/.

5   Congressional Budget Office, "The Budget and Economic Outlook: 2023 to 2033," February 15, 2023, https://www.cbo.gov/publication/58848, CBO, Budget and Economic Data, Revenue Projections, by Category, https://www.cbo.gov/data/budget-economic-data#7

6   Congressional Budget Office, "Monthly Budget Review: September 2023," Oct. 10, 2023, https://www.cbo.gov/publication/59544; William McBride, "Federal Deficit Grew to $2 Trillion in FY 2023," Oct. 12, 2023, https://taxfoundation.org/blog/federal-budget-deficit-2023/

new claims due to rampant fraud. Individual income tax refunds were $129 billion higher this year than last, a 52 percent increase. Another factor behind the decline, as noted by the CBO, is that the IRS postponed the filing deadline for taxpayers affected by natural disasters, including most taxpayers in California, until October 16 or later.

In contrast, payroll taxes grew 9 percent to $1.6 trillion in FY 2023, reflecting growth in wages and jobs. Corporate income taxes were roughly flat, falling $5 billion, or 1 percent, to $420 billion, despite the introduction of the new minimum tax on corporate book income and the stock buyback tax, both part of the Inflation Reduction Act (IRA) enacted last year. Other receipts dropped $124 billion, or 35 percent, to $232 billion in FY 2023, primarily reflecting a near-zeroing out of remittances from the Federal Reserve as higher interest rates caused the central bank's interest expense to offset its income.

The extreme volatility in revenue collections over the last two years, marked by extraordinary capital gains in 2021 and most likely heavy losses in 2022, reflects a federal tax system that is heavily reliant on high-income investors (where capital gains and losses are concentrated), as we will see in more detail in the next section. It also means that future tax collections will depend a great deal on fluctuations in the economy, including the ups and downs of the stock market. As one indicator, the S&P 500 rose about 27 percent in 2021, dropped about 19 percent in 2022, and is up about 14 percent this year. This, and other one-time factors mentioned above, suggests FY 2024 collections may be closer to FY 2022 levels than FY 2023 levels.

Federal Tax Revenue above Historical Averages in Recent Years and Expected to Remain So under Current Law

Federal Tax Revenue as a Share of GDP

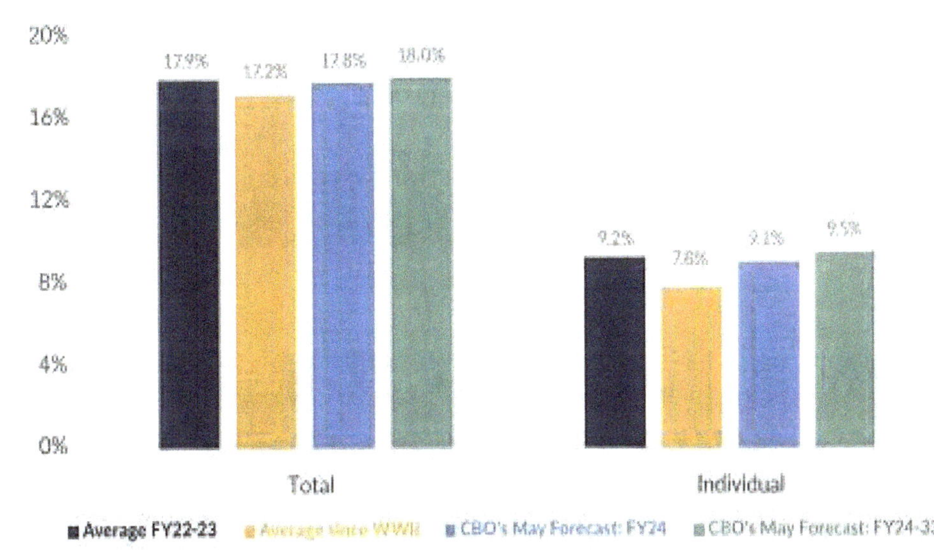

Source: CBO, OMB, BEA.

Simply averaging FY 2022 and FY 2023 together yields total federal tax collections of 17.9 percent of GDP, which is 0.7 percentage points above the historical average since WWII. Individual income tax collections average to 9.2 percent of GDP over the last two years, which is about 1.4 percentage points above the historical average. In addition, federal tax collections exhibit an upward trend resulting from many of the provisions of the Tax Cuts and Jobs Act (TCJA), including the phaseout of bonus depreciation that is set to occur over the next five years and the expiration of the individual income tax provisions at the end of 2025, as well as the permanent features that boost economic growth, especially the lower corporate tax rate.[7] As such, under a current law baseline, we expect federal tax collections over the next several years to trend upwards towards 18 percent of GDP or higher, whereas full or partial extension of TCJA's expiring provisions would reduce revenue to a range of about 17 to 18 percent of GDP.[8] Under current law, the CBO projects total collections of 18.0 percent of GDP and individual income tax collections of 9.5 percent of GDP on average from FY 2024 to FY 2033.[9]

Most of the Federal Tax Burden Is Paid by High Earners

By any objective measure, the U.S. tax code is extremely progressive and very redistributive. According to the latest IRS data for 2020, the top 5 percent of taxpayers (about 7.9 million filers who earn more than $220,521) paid in aggregate $1.1 trillion in income taxes, amounting to 62.7 percent of all income taxes paid that year.[10] The top 1 percent of taxpayers (about 1.6 million filers who earn more than $548,336) paid $723 billion in income taxes, or 42.3 percent of all income taxes paid—a larger share than the bottom 95 percent of taxpayers combined.

The share of federal income taxes paid by the top 1 percent is higher than it has been in at least 20 years, according to IRS data.[11] In 2001, the top 1 percent's share of income taxes paid was 33.2 percent, then fluctuated with the business cycle and the ups and downs of the housing and stock markets, before rising steadily to its current high of 42.3 percent in 2020. The top 1 percent's share of income taxes could well go higher in 2021 and 2022 due to growth of capital gains revenue, which is paid primarily by high earners.

High income taxpayers also pay the highest tax rates, according to the IRS. The average income tax rate in 2020 was 13.6 percent. The top 5 percent of taxpayers paid a 22.4 percent average rate while the top 1 percent of taxpayers paid a 26.0 percent average rate—more than eight times higher than the 3.1 percent average rate paid by the bottom half of taxpayers. The top 0.001 percent, or the richest 1,575 tax returns filed in 2020, paid nearly $71 billion in income taxes and had an average tax rate of 23.7 percent.

7   Tax Foundation, "Preliminary Details and Analysis of the Tax Cuts and Jobs Act," Dec. 18, 2017, https://taxfoundation.org/research/all/federal/final-tax-cuts-and-jobs-act-details-analysis/; William McBride and Alex Durante, "New Study Finds TCJA Strongly Boosted Corporate Investment," Tax Foundation, Oct. 21, 2023, https://taxfoundation.org/blog/tcja-corporate-tax-economic-effects/.

8   Our recent modeling of potential extensions of TCJA expiring provisions indicates full extension of all provisions as they were in 2021, including individual, estate, and business provisions, would reduce revenue to about 17 percent of GDP on average from FY 2024 to FY 2033 (dynamically scored, i.e., accounting for the policy's impacts on economic growth) whereas extension of only the business provisions would reduce revenue to about 17.7 percent of GDP.

9   CBO, "An Update to the Budget Outlook: 2023 to 2033," May 12, 2023, https://www.cbo.gov/publication/59096.

10 Internal Revenue Service, Statistics of Income, "Number of Returns, Shares of AGI and Total Income Tax, AGI Floor on Percentiles in Current and Constant Dollars, and Average Tax Rates," Table 1, and "Number of Returns, Shares of AGI and Total Income Tax, and Average Tax Rates," Table 2, https://www.irs.gov/statistics/soi-tax-stats-individual-income-tax-rates-and-tax-shares; Erica York, "Summary of the Latest Federal Income Tax Data, 2023 Update," Tax Foundation, Jan. 26, 2023, https://taxfoundation.org/publications/latest-federal-income-tax-data/.

11 Erica York, "Summary of the Latest Federal Income Tax Data, 2023 Update," Tax Foundation, Jan. 26, 2023, https://taxfoundation.org/publications/latest-federal-income-tax-data/

The Top 1 Percent's Share of Income Taxes Has Increased Over Time

Shares of Income Taxes by Income Group, 2001-2020

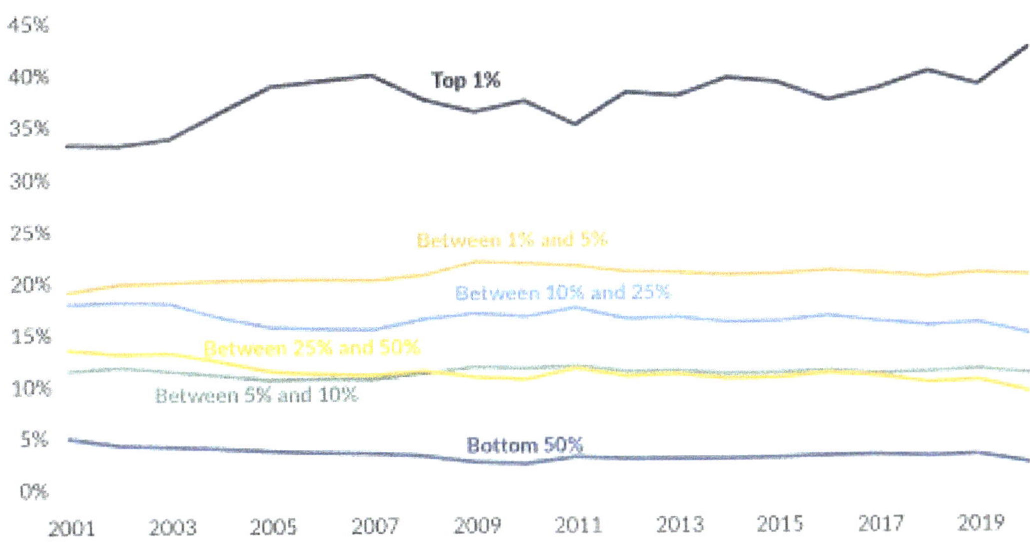

Source: IRS, Statistics of Income, Individual Income Rates and Tax Shares.

The average tax rate for the top 0.001 percent is slightly lower than that of the top 1 percent because a larger share of the top 0.001 percent's income is capital gains, which face a lower rate schedule. One justification for the lower rate is that capital gains income is earned in an environment where other taxes have already been applied. In particular, shareholder taxes on capital gains and dividends essentially apply on top of the corporate income tax of 21 percent. That is, the same dollar of corporate income is first taxed by the corporate income tax and then taxed again when distributed to shareholders in the form of capital gains and dividends. Note that the shares and average tax rates cited above do not reflect the additional burden of the corporate income tax.[12]

Analysis from the CBO provides a more complete picture of the distribution of the federal tax burden. When accounting for individual income taxes—including the outlay portion of refundable tax credits—corporate income taxes, payroll taxes, estate taxes, and excise taxes, CBO finds that the federal tax system, as a whole, is progressive. [13] The latest data indicates that households in the highest income quintile paid about 69 percent of all federal taxes in 2019, and the top 1 percent of households paid about 25 percent of all federal taxes.[14] In contrast, the bottom quintile of households paid about 0.1 percent of all federal taxes.

---

12   The IRS statistics on shares and average tax rates also do not include the outlay portion of refundable tax credits, such as the Earned Income Tax Credit (EITC) and the Child Tax Credit (CTC), which if included would reduce further the average tax rates paid by low-income filers and increase the share of federal income taxes paid by high-income filers.

13   Congressional Budget Office, "The Distribution of Household Income 2019," Nov. 15, 2022, https://www.cbo.gov/system/files/2022-11/58353-HouseholdIncome.pdf; Garrett Watson, "CBO Analysis Finds Income Growth and Progressive Tax Code in 2019," Tax Foundation, Jan. 10, 2023, https://taxfoundation.org/us-income-growth-progressive-tax-code/.

14   In CBO's analysis, the top 1 percent income group represents about 1.2 million households. Income thresholds defining each income group vary by household size. For example, a one person household in the top 1 percent of income earns more than $447,200 in 2019 while a four person household in the top 1 percent earns more than $894,400.

High-Income Taxpayers Paid the Highest Average Income Tax Rates

Average Federal Income Tax Rate by Income Group, 2020

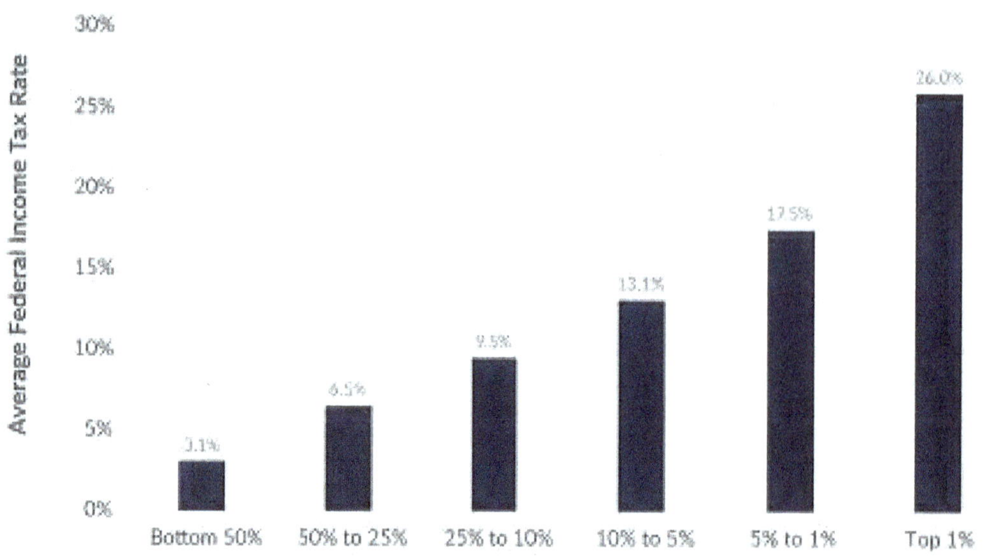

Source: IRS, Statistics of Income, Individual Income Rates and Tax Shares

Like the IRS data on federal income taxes, the CBO analysis indicates the share of all federal taxes paid by high earners has grown over time. For example, the share of federal taxes paid by households in the top 1 percent has approximately doubled to about 25 percent in 2019 from roughly 12 percent in the early 1980s.

The Top 1 Percent Pays About 25 Percent of All Federal Taxes

Shares of Federal Taxes, 1979 to 2019

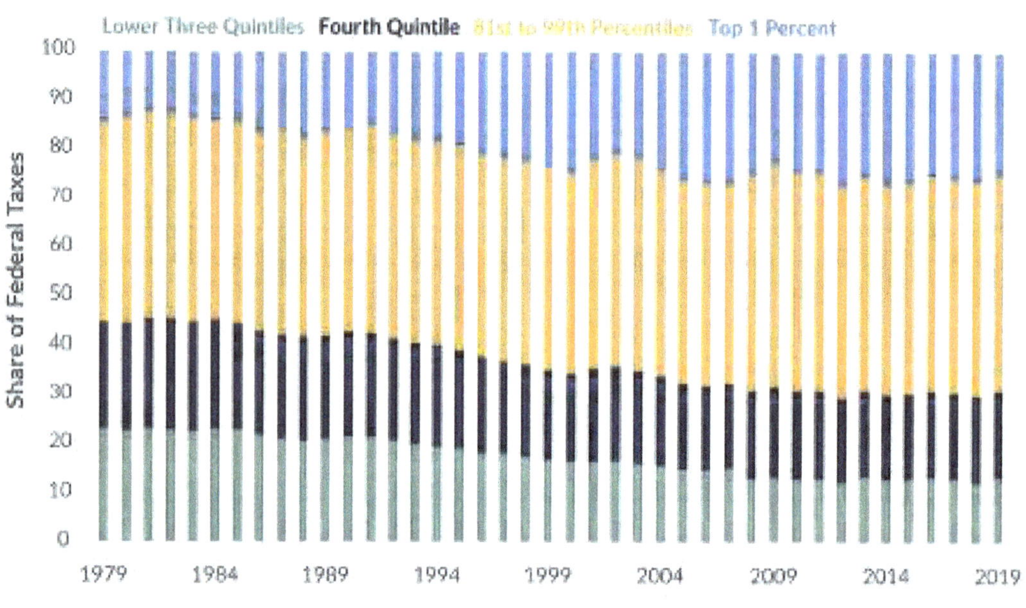

Source: Congressional Budget Office, "The Distribution of Household Income, 2019," Exhibit 16

Furthermore, the CBO analysis indicates that average federal tax rates increase substantially with income. For example, the top quintile of households paid an average federal tax rate of 24.4 percent in 2019 and the top 1 percent of households paid an average federal tax rate of 30.0 percent. In contrast, the bottom quintile paid an average federal tax rate of 0.5 percent, reflecting the fact that refundable tax credits for this group almost entirely offset payroll taxes and other federal taxes.

The CBO notes that within the top 1 percent's average federal tax rates are relatively flat at about 30 percent, as the effect of lower capital gains tax rates are offset by higher average corporate tax rates.[15] For example, the top 0.01 percent of households paid an average federal tax rate of 30.2 percent in 2019.

Over time, the average federal tax rate paid by the top 1 percent has remained within a range of about 25 to 35 percent since 1979, and as of 2019 is about in the middle of that range and close to the average of 30.5 percent over the period 1979 to 2019. However, the average federal tax rate for the bottom quintile has declined substantially, to nearly zero in 2019 due to the introduction and expansion of refundable tax credits from a high of about 12 percent in 1984.

Average Federal Tax Rates Vary Highly by Tax Type and Income Level and are Progressive Overall

Average Federal Tax Rates by Tax Source, 2019

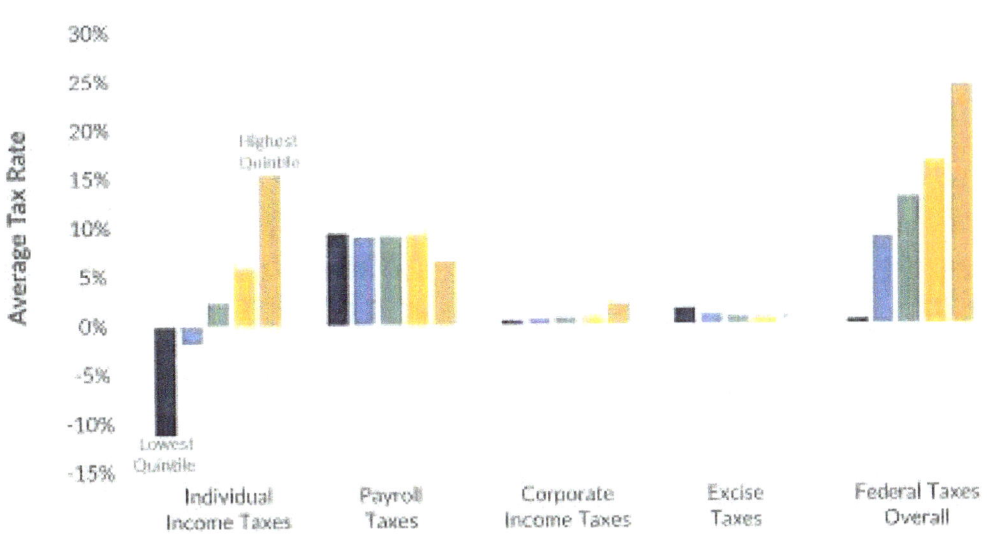

* The highest quintile has an effective federal excise tax rate between 0 and 0.5 percent.
Source: Congressional Budget Office, "The Distribution of Household Income, 2019," Exhibit 13.

Data from the Joint Committee on Taxation (JCT) confirms that average federal tax rates consistently rise with income. When including all federal taxes, the bottom 50 percent of taxpayers face an average federal tax rate of 6.3 percent, compared to an average rate of 24.8 percent for the top 1 percent of taxpayers. The federal income tax is the most progressive of the federal taxes, with corporate income taxes and estate and gift taxes also adding to federal progressivity. The progressive tax sources more than offset

---

15 In CBO's analysis, 75 percent of corporate income taxes are allocated to owners of capital in proportion to their income from interest, dividends, rents, and adjusted capital gains, and 25 percent to workers in proportion to their labor income.

payroll taxes and excise taxes that apply higher average tax rates to lower income groups. The JCT data also shows average federal taxes rise within the top 1 percent, from an average tax rate of 22.6 percent for those in the 99th to 99.5th percentiles of income to 32.9 percent for the top 0.01 percent of earners, representing about 15,000 taxpayers in the United States.

Average Federal Tax Rates Vary Highly by Tax Type and Income Level and are Progressive Overall

Average Federal Tax Rates by Tax Source and Income Group by Percentile, 2018

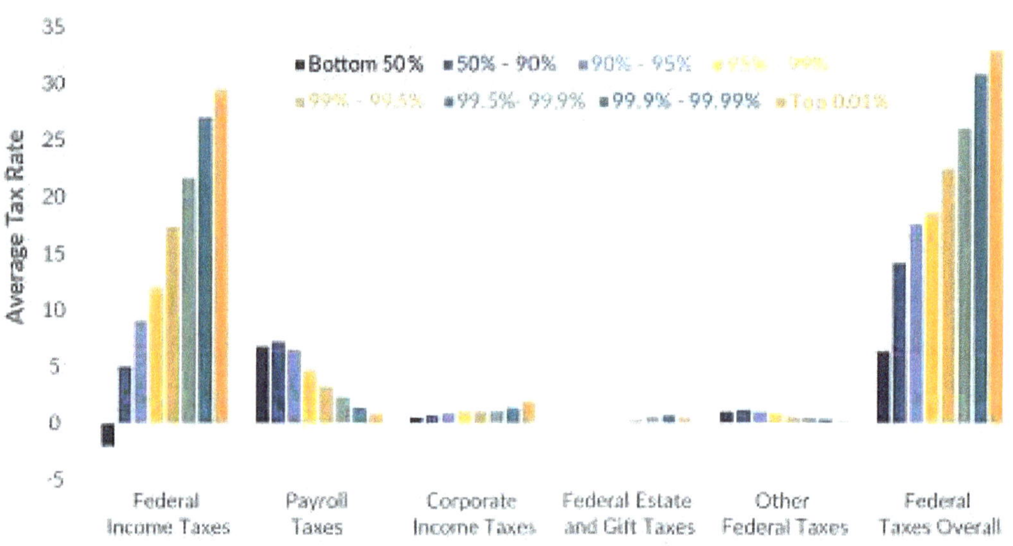

Source. JCT. Other federal taxes are mostly excise taxes and customs duties.

Tax Code's Complexity Adds to the Burden

By any measure, the federal tax code is extremely complex. Totaling more than 6,000 pages and about 4 million words (plus about 15,000 pages of associated tax law interpretations), no taxpayer can reasonably be expected to fully comprehend it.[16] The complexity derives in part from the basic challenge of defining and taxing income, an endeavor the country embarked on more than 100 years ago. Every Congress and administration since has revised and added to an accumulating pile of deductions, credits, and special provisions. By official measures, there are now more than 200 such special provisions known as "tax expenditures," costing about $2 trillion annually. In the last three years alone more than 100 tax expenditures have been created or amended.[17]

16   Demian Brady, "Tax Complexity 2021: Compliance Burdens Ease for Third Year Since Tax Reform," NTU, April 15, 2021, https://www.ntu.org/foundation/detail/tax-complexity-2021-compliance-burdens-ease-for-third-year-since-tax-reform.
17   The Joint Committee on Taxation, "Estimates of Federal Tax Expenditures for Fiscal Years 2022-2026," Dec. 22, 2022, https://www.jct.gov/publications/2022/jcx-22-22/; Treasury Department, "Tax Expenditures" https://home.treasury.gov/policy-issues/tax-policy/tax-expenditures

While some tax expenditures are important structural elements of the tax code, many are complicated and disproportionately benefit specific industries or types of households.[18] The CBO finds about half of the total income tax benefits of expenditures go to high-income households.[19]

The Inflation Reduction Act (IRA), enacted last year, adds several complicated provisions to the tax code, including a book minimum tax, a stock buyback tax, and more than 20 different tax subsidies for green energy. All of these require extensive regulatory guidance which continues to roll out even as much of the law took effect at the beginning of this year.[20] Taxpayers, too, have highlighted several remaining concerns and ambiguities in the law (e.g., reporting requirements and applicable financial statements for the book minimum tax, and domestic content rules for the green energy tax credits).[21]

The uncertainty in the law also translates into uncertainty about the budgetary costs and distributional impacts. For example, researchers now estimate the budgetary cost of the IRA's green energy credits and subsidies will exceed $1 trillion over a decade, three times the original cost estimated by the CBO and the JCT, with the benefits accruing mainly to high earners.[22]

In the same month the IRA was enacted, Congress passed the CHIPS and Science Act, which provides billions of dollars of targeted (and complex) incentives and investment tax credits for semiconductor manufacturing, along with a variety of eligibility and reporting requirements.[23]

In 2022 (before the IRA or the CHIPS Act), Americans spent more than 6.5 billion hours trying to comply with the tax code, according to the latest estimates from the White House Office of Information and Regulatory Affairs (OIRA).[24] Based on wage and benefit estimates for tax preparers and certified public accountants, we estimate the hourly compliance costs of the tax code equates to about $313 billion each year in lost productivity, or 1.4 percent of GDP.[25] The compliance burden for individual taxpayers is nearly $74 billion annually, while the burden on corporate entities of complying with just their income tax returns is more than $60 billion. Much of the remaining $179 billion of costs comes from complying with hundreds of other business tax forms and regulations, such as those relating to depreciation and amortization. Compliance with income tax returns for estates and trusts costs $18 billion a year, approaching the amount of tax revenue raised by the estate tax.

18　Alex Muresianu, "JCT Tax Expenditure Report: Not All Expenditures Are Created Equal," Tax Foundation, Feb. 13, 2023, https://taxfoundation.org/largest-tax-expenditures-saving-investment-tax/; Erica York and William McBride, "Lawmakers Could Pay for Reconciliation While Improving the Tax Code," Tax Foundation, Oct. 25, 2021, https://taxfoundation.org/pay-for-reconciliation-tax/.

19　Congressional Budget Office, "Distribution of Major Expenditures in 2019," October 2021, https://www.cbo.gov/system/files/2021-10/5/413-TaxExpenditures.pdf.

20　William McBride, Alex Muresianu, Erica York, and Michael Hartt, "Inflation Reduction Act One Year After Enactment," Tax Foundation, Aug. 16, 2023, https://taxfoundation.org/research/all/federal/inflation-reduction-act-taxes/; Internal Revenue Service, "Latest Updates on the Inflation Reduction Act of 2022," https://www.irs.gov/inflation-reduction-act-of-2022.

21　William McBride, Alex Muresianu, Erica York, and Michael Hartt, "Inflation Reduction Act One Year After Enactment," Tax Foundation, Aug. 16, 2023, https://taxfoundation.org/research/all/federal/inflation-reduction-act-taxes/.

22　Ibid; John Bistline, Neil Mehrotra, and Catherine Wolfram, "Economic Implications of the Climate Provisions of the Inflation Reduction Act," Brookings Papers on Economic Activity, March 2023, https://www.brookings.edu/wp-content/uploads/2023/03/BPEA_Spring2023_Bistline-et-al_unembargoedUpdated.pdf; Jason Furman, "Comment on 'Economic Implications of the Climate Provisions of the Inflation Reduction Act,'" Mar. 30, 2023, https://www.brookings.edu/wp-content/uploads/2023/02/2b_20230330-BPEA-climate-furman-comment.pdf; Christine McDaniel, "The Cost of Battery Production Tax Credits Provided in the IRA," Forbes, Feb. 1, 2023, https://www.forbes.com/sites/christinemcdaniel/2023/02/01/the-cost-of-battery-production-tax-credits-provided-in-the-ira/?sh=352fc62279ef; Christine McDaniel, "The Costs of Wind Production Tax Credits Provided in the IRA," Forbes, Mar. 8, 2023, https://www.forbes.com/sites/christinemcdaniel/2023/03/08/the-costs-of-wind-production-tax-credits-provided-in-the-ira/?sh=7cd64295ff7; Goldman Sachs, "Carbonomics: The Third American Energy Revolution," Mar. 22, 2023.

23　Erica York, "Careful What You Wish For: CHIPS Subsidies Require 'Excess Profits' Sharing," Tax Foundation, Mar. 2, 2023, https://taxfoundation.org/biden-semiconductor-chips-act-subsidies/.

24　White House Office of Information and Regulatory Affairs, Information Collection Review, https://www.reginfo.gov/public/do/PRAMain.

25　Scott Hodge, "The Tax Compliance Costs of IRS Regulations," Tax Foundation, Aug. 23, 2022, https://taxfoundation.org/tax-compliance-costs-irs-regulations/

Our estimate of compliance costs does not include the cost of tax planning, which is a significant industry on its own. Nor does it include the cost of uncertainty in the law for taxpayers, which makes planning for taxes as well as investment and other economic activities difficult and costly.

The majority of the compliance burden is from the complex taxing of business income, which involves tracking and reporting multiple items of income and expense to arrive at net taxable income and allowing offsets from net income to account for past losses (in a typical year roughly 40 percent of companies are in a loss position).[26] In addition, the U.S. tax code contains several business credits, exclusions, and other special provisions that increase compliance costs. Multinational corporations face a slew of complex provisions that subject various types of foreign income and cross-border transactions to tax, including Subpart F, Global Intangible Low-Taxed Income (GILTI), Foreign-Derived Intangible Income (FDII), and Base Erosion and Anti-Abuse Tax (BEAT).[27]

For individual filers, compliance costs generally increase proportionally with income, such that most of the compliance burden is borne by high earners.[28] High earning individuals typically have multiple sources of income beyond wages, including capital gains, dividends, rents, royalties, and pass-through business income from partnerships and S corporations (income from these business forms is subject to individual income tax rather than corporate income tax).

Another aspect of the tax code's complexity is the administrative costs and challenges for the IRS, an agency whose responsibilities have grown well beyond simple revenue collection to include administration of subsidies and benefits relating to children, health care, education, housing, energy, the environment, economic stimulus, and more.[29] Pursuant to its expanded role, in FY 2021 the IRS processed some 261 million returns and forms and received some 4.7 billion pieces of information, detailing the composition and activities of nearly every American household and business.[30] In recent years, the IRS has found itself literally buried in paperwork, resulting in processing delays, millions of returns backlogged, and poor customer service.[31] Last year, for instance, the IRS answered only about 13 percent of the 173 million phone calls it received from taxpayers asking for help; those who got through waited an average of 29 minutes.[32]

IRS customer service improved considerably this filing season, due partly to reduced demand as many complicated pandemic-era policies expired, such as the 2021 expanded child tax credit, as well as new funding from the IRA and a shift in resources towards phone service.[33] For example, call volume dropped by more than half, returning to "normal" levels seen pre-pandemic in which the IRS received some 30

26 Arthur P. Hall, "House Way & Means Committee Testimony: Compliance Costs of Alternative Tax Systems II," Tax Foundation, March 1996, https://files.taxfoundation.org/legacy/docs/8926e37c5827f958604933276fcb4864.pdf?_gl=1*1bccc81*_ga*MjkzNjU2MTcuMTY4MDg2NjcxOA.*_ga_FP7KWDV08V*MTY4MTI5MzY4Ni40ljEuMTY4MTI5Mzcz Ny45LjAuMA

27 Kyle Pomerleau, "A Hybrid Approach: The Treatment of Foreign Profits under the Tax Cuts and Jobs Act," Tax Foundation, May 3, 2018, https://taxfoundation.org/treatment-foreign-profits-tax-cuts-jobs-act/.

28 Daniel Berger, Eric Toder, Victoria Bryant, John Guyton, and Patrick Langetieg, "Estimating the Effects of Tax Reform on Compliance Burdens," Urban Institute, May 19, 2018, https://www.urban.org/research/publication/estimating-effects-tax-reform-compliance-burdens.

29 Alex Muresianu and Garrett Watson, "Chaotic IRS Filing Season Shows the Perils of Running Social Policy Through the Tax Code," Tax Foundation, Apr. 18, 2022, https://taxfoundation.org/irs-filing-season-2022/.

30 Internal Revenue Service, Data Book 2021, May 2022, https://www.irs.gov/statistics/soi-tax-stats-irs-data-book; Joseph Bishop-Henchman, "Transforming the Internal Revenue Service," Cato Institute, Apr. 11, 2023, https://www.cato.org/policy-analysis/transforming-internal-revenue-service/.

31 Internal Revenue Service National Taxpayer Advocate, "2022 Annual Report to Congress," Jan. 11, 2023, https://www.taxpayeradvocate.irs.gov/news/national-taxpayer-advocate-delivers-2022-annual-report-to-congress/; Joseph Bishop-Henchman, "Transforming the Internal Revenue Service," Cato Institute, Apr. 11, 2023, https://www.cato.org/policy-analysis/transforming-internal-revenue-service/.

32 Internal Revenue Service National Taxpayer Advocate, "2022 Annual Report to Congress," Jan. 11, 2023, https://www.taxpayeradvocate.irs.gov/news/national-taxpayer-advocate-delivers-2022-annual-report-to-congress/.

33 Erin Collins, "Objectives Report to Congress, Fiscal Year 2024," National Taxpayer Advocate, June 2023, https://www.taxpayeradvocate.irs.gov/reports/2024-objectives-report-to-congress/; William McBride, Alex Muresianu, Erica York, and Michael Hartt, "Inflation Reduction Act One Year After Enactment," Tax Foundation, Aug. 16, 2023, https://taxfoundation.org/research/all/federal/inflation-reduction-act-taxes/.

million to 40 million calls from taxpayers during the filing season. The IRS answered about 34 percent of calls this filing season and substantially reduced wait times. In addition, the IRS was able to significantly reduce its backlog of returns.

However, other performance metrics worsened, including longer processing delays for taxpayer correspondence and amended returns. As well, the number of backlogged identity theft cases increased 46 percent to about 465,000 as of April, requiring about 15 months to resolve on average.[34] Making matters worse, some aspects of the tax code became more complex, consuming more IRS resources and detracting from other core duties. For instance, earlier this year, the IRS requested an additional $3.9 billion in funding to further implement the IRA's green energy tax credits.[35] Clearly, there is room for further improvement, as an overly complex tax code presents ongoing administrative challenges at the IRS that are also problematic for taxpayers.

A report from the Government Accountability Office (GAO) sheds light on the challenges faced by the IRS and taxpayers as a result of the increasing complexity of the code.[36] The report finds that the average number of hours the IRS spends per audit has increased about 30 percent in recent years, to 6.5 hours in 2021 from 5.0 hours in 2010. The increase is concentrated in high-income returns. Average hours per audit increased 209 percent for incomes of $5 million and above, to about 58 hours in 2021 from about 19 hours per return in 2010. Average hours per audit increased 118 percent for incomes between $500,000 and $5 million, to 34 hours from about 16, and 103 percent for incomes between $200,000 and $500,000, from about 10 to 21 hours. In contrast, audits for incomes below $200,000 took considerably less time—about 2 hours on average for incomes below $25,000, and 6 hours for incomes between $25,000 and $200,000, and this remained stable over this period.

The GAO report notes that IRS officials attribute the increase in average audit hours to "greater complexity of higher-income audits and increased case transfers due to auditor attrition." The GAO report mentions several legislative changes that have added to the IRS's responsibilities in recent years, including the Patient Protection and Affordable Care Act, the Foreign Account Tax Compliance Act, the TCJA, as well as some 496 million stimulus payments totaling $837 billion as part of the CARES Act and other pandemic relief packages. (Note the GAO report was published before enactment of the IRA or CHIPS Act.)

As a measure of the efficiency of audits, or the "bang for the buck," the GAO compared the recommended additional tax with hours spent on audits. The GAO found that audits of the highest income returns—those with income of $5 million or more—resulted in the highest amounts of recommended additional tax per audit hour ($4,880 in 2021), followed by audits of those claiming the EITC ($3,130) and those reporting less than $25,000 of income ($2,120). In aggregate, the majority of the total recommended additional tax came from audits of taxpayers with income below $200,000. On average, roughly half of recommended additional amounts are ultimately collected, however the collection rate for EITC returns exceeds 70 percent since these audits are typically done prior to issuing refunds.

34   Erin Collins, "Objectives Report to Congress, Fiscal Year 2024," National Taxpayer Advocate, June 2023, https://www.taxpayeradvocate.irs.gov/reports/2024-objectives-report-to-congress/.
35   Internal Revenue Service, "Inflation Reduction Act Strategic Operating Plan," Apr. 5, 2023, https://www.irs.gov/pub/irs-pdf/p3744.pdf
36   Government Accountability Office, "Tax Compliance: Trends of IRS Audit Rates and Results for Individual Taxpayers by Income," May 17, 2022, https://www.gao.gov/products/gao-22-104960.

Lastly, the GAO report documents that audit rates for individual income tax returns have decreased for all income levels, dropping to 0.25 percent in 2019 from an average of 0.9 percent in 2010, which IRS officials attribute mainly to reduced staffing as a result of reduced funding. Audit rates decreased the most for high earners because, according to IRS officials, these audits are generally more complex and require more staff time to complete.

Simplifying the tax code would reduce IRS resources required to more effectively administer it, including by reducing the time needed to audit the currently complex returns of high earners. A simpler tax code would also reduce taxpayer confusion so that there would be less need for the IRS to produce volumes of guidance and respond to millions of taxpayer calls for assistance. Less confusion on the part of taxpayers would also boost compliance.[37] As the IRS Taxpayer Advocate explains: "Simplifying the Code and eliminating complexities in the IRS's procedures would reduce taxpayer compliance burdens by making it easier for taxpayers to understand their filing and payment obligations, and it would also make it easier for the IRS to administer the tax laws. Thus, simplification is essential to the integrity of the U.S. tax system and will enhance voluntary compliance."[38]

The Economic Cost of High Marginal Income Tax Rates

Decades of economic research amply demonstrates the steep cost of high marginal income tax rates that arises from disincentives to work, save, and invest.[39] The economic harm of income taxes increases with the square of the tax rate, meaning high income tax rates come with a disproportionately large additional excess burden. This burden is over and above the tax revenue collected, manifesting itself over the course of several years as a drag on economic growth through less investment, less innovation, fewer jobs, and lower wages.[40]

A study based on postwar tax reforms in the United States found that reducing marginal tax rates on individual income for the top 1 percent of earners leads to increases in real GDP and declines in unemployment, with a 1 percentage point cut in the tax rate increasing real GDP by 0.78 percent by the third year after the tax change.[41] Given the size of the U.S. economy today, that equates to about $204 billion in additional GDP for each 1 percentage point cut in the marginal tax rate on individual income earned by the top 1 percent. The study shows the benefits of the resulting economic growth would be felt throughout the economy.

In looking at the experience of developed countries over the period 1971 to 2004, researchers at the Organisation of for Economic Co-operation and Development (OECD) concluded that "a reduction in the

37 Garrett Watson, "Closing the Tax Gap and Improving the Tax Code Are Complementary Goals," Tax Foundation, November 21, 2019, https://taxfoundation.org/closing-tax-gap-improving-tax-code/

38 Erin Collins, "Objectives Report to Congress, Fiscal Year 2024," National Taxpayer Advocate, June 2023, https://www.taxpayeradvocate.irs.gov/reports/2024-objectives-report-to-congress/

39 N. Gregory Mankiw, Matthew Weinzierl, and Danny Yagan, "Optimal Taxation in Theory and Practice," Journal of Economic Perspectives 2009, volume 23(4), https://eml.berkeley.edu/~yagan/OptimalTaxation.pdf; William McBride, "What is the Evidence on Taxes and Growth," Tax Foundation, Dec. 18, 2012, https://www.taxfoundation.org/what-evidence-taxes-and-growth/; Alex Durante, "Reviewing Recent Evidence of the Effect of Taxes on Economic Growth," Tax Foundation, May 2021, https://taxfoundation.org/reviewing-recent-evidence-effect-taxes-economic-growth/; Timothy Vermeer, "The Impact of Individual Income Tax Changes on Economic Growth," Tax Foundation, June 14, 2022, https://taxfoundation.org/income-taxes-affect-economy/.

40 Robert Carroll, "The Excess Burden of Taxes and the Economic Cost of High Tax Rates," Tax Foundation, August 2009, https://files.taxfoundation.org/legacy/docs/sr170.pdf; Martin Feldstein, "Tax Avoidance and the Deadweight Loss of the Income Tax," The Review of Economics and Statistics 81.4 (November 1999): 674-680, https://www.jstor.org/stable/2646716.

41 Karel Mertens and José Luis Montiel Olea, "Marginal Tax Rates and Income: New Time Series Evidence," The Quarterly Journal of Economics 133.4 (November 2018), https://academic.oup.com/qje/article-abstract/133/4/1803/4880451?redirectedFrom=fulltext.

top marginal [individual] tax rate is found to raise productivity in industries with potentially high rates of enterprise creation. Thus, reducing top marginal tax rates may help to enhance economy-wide productivity in OECD countries with a large share of such industries."[42]

The CBO modeled three types of tax increases to fund a permanent increase in government spending of 10 percent of GDP annually: a flat labor tax, a flat income tax, and a progressive income tax. The CBO found that a progressive income tax is the most economically damaging of the three options, reducing GDP by 10 percent after 10 years, and reducing lifetime consumption and hours worked, especially for younger households.[43]

Corporate income taxes are generally more economically damaging than individual income taxes, since they make investment opportunities less profitable on an after-tax basis for corporations, reducing the likelihood that marginal investments will be pursued. In most countries including the U.S., business investment makes up the bulk of all private sector investment; more uniquely in the U.S., about half of business investment is done by corporations and the other half by pass-through businesses subject to individual income taxes.

An OECD study examining data from 63 countries concluded that corporate income taxes are the most economically damaging way to raise revenue, followed by individual income taxes, consumption taxes, and property taxes.[44] A study on taxes in the United Kingdom found that taxes on consumption are less economically damaging than taxes on corporate and individual income.[45] A study of U.S. tax changes since World War II found that a 1 percentage point cut in the average corporate tax rate raises real GDP per capita by 0.6 percent after one year, a somewhat larger impact than a similarly sized cut in individual income taxes.[46] Based on U.S. state taxes, a study found that a 1 percentage point cut in the corporate tax rate leads to a 0.2 percent increase in employment and a 0.3 percent increase in wages.[47]

Furthermore, several studies demonstrate that the corporate tax is borne in part by workers.[48] For instance, a study of corporate taxes in Germany found that workers bear about half of the tax burden in the form of lower wages, with low-skilled, young, and female employees disproportionately harmed.[49]

The corporate tax is also borne by owners of shares, including retirees earning considerably less than $400,000. In the short run, the JCT assumes owners of capital bear all of the corporate tax, yet that includes more than 90 million tax filers earning less than $200,000. In the long run, the JCT assumes

42 Åsa Johansson, Christopher Heady, Jens Arnold, Bert Brys, Cyrille Schwellnus, & Laura Vartia, "Taxation and Economic Growth."
43 Congressional Budget Office, "The Economics of Financing a Large and Permanent Increase in Government Spending: Working Paper 2021-03," Mar. 22, 2021, https://www.cbo.gov/publication/57021; see also Garrett Watson, "Congressional Budget Office and Tax Foundation Modeling Show That Some Tax Hikes Are More Damaging Than Others," Tax Foundation, Mar. 26, 2021, https://www.taxfoundation.org/tax-hikes-are-more-damaging-than-others-analysis/.
44 Åsa Johansson, Christopher Heady, Jens Matthias Arnold, Bert Brys, and Laura Vartia, "Taxation and Economic Growth," Organisation for Economic Co-Operation and Development Working Paper No. 620, July 3, 2008, https://www.oecd-library.org/economics/taxation-and-economic-growth_241216205486.
45 Ahn D. M. Nguyen, Luisanna Onnis, and Raffaele Rossi, "The Macroeconomic Effects of Income and Consumption Tax Changes," American Economic Journal: Economic Policy 13:2 (May 2021), https://www.aeaweb.org/articles?id=10.1257/pol.20170241&&from=f
46 Karel Mertens and Morten O. Ravn, "The Dynamic Effects of Personal and Corporate Income Tax Changes in the United States," American Economic Review 103:4 (June 2013), https://www.aeaweb.org/articles?id=10.1257/aer.103.4.1212.
47 Alexander Ljungqvist and Michael Smolyansky, "To Cut or Not to Cut? On the Impact of Corporate Taxes on Employment and Income," National Bureau of Economic Research Working Paper No. 20753 (October 2018), https://www.nber.org/system/files/working_papers/w20753/w20753.pdf.
48 Stephen J. Entin, "Labor Bears Much of the Cost of the Corporate Tax," Tax Foundation, Oct. 24, 2017, https://www.taxfoundation.org/labor-bears-corporate-tax/; and Alex Durante, "Who Bears the Burden of Corporate Taxation? A Review of Recent Evidence," June 10, 2021, https://www.taxfoundation.org/who-bears-burden-corporate-tax/
49 Clemens Fuest, Andreas Peichl, and Sebastian Siegloch, "Do Higher Corporate Taxes Reduce Wages? Micro Evidence from Germany," American Economic Review 108:2 (February 2018), 393–418, https://www.doi.org/10.1257/aer.20130570

workers bear a portion of the corporate tax, such that the burden falls on more than 150 million tax filers earning less than $200,000.[50]

Another factor to consider regarding the corporate tax in particular is competitiveness with respect to our major trading partners, as corporate investment is highly mobile internationally and will flow to lower tax locations all else equal. The corporate tax rate reduction from the TCJA brought the U.S. closer to the average among developed countries accounting for federal and state level taxes, though it remains slightly above average. The U.S. combined federal-state corporate tax rate in 2022 was 25.8 percent, compared to 21.2 percent in the average EU country and 23.6 percent in the average OECD country.[51]

Lastly, one of the most problematic and economically destructive aspects of the U.S. tax code is the double taxation of corporate income by the corporate income tax (and now also the book minimum tax) and shareholder taxes on capital gains and dividends. Accounting for federal and state corporate and individual incomes taxes, the top integrated tax rate on corporate income distributed as dividends is about 47 percent in the U.S., compared to an OECD average of about 42 percent.[52] Several OECD countries have integrated corporate and individual tax codes to eliminate or reduce the negative effects of double taxation of corporate income. In the U.S., after decades of double taxing corporate income, a large share of business activity has migrated to pass-through form, which has only one layer of income tax as owners report pass-through profits on their individual income tax returns.[53]

Recommendations for Reform

For several years, the Tax Foundation has observed and analyzed tax systems from around the world and evaluated them based on the principles of sound tax policy.[54] Most tax policy experts agree that taxes should be simple, transparent, and stable over time so they are easy to understand, comply with, and administer. Another element of sound tax policy is neutrality: the tax code should generally treat taxpayers equally with minimum preferences, which extends to equal treatment of immediate versus delayed consumption via saving. A tax code that embodies these principles naturally supports economic flourishing, including plentiful jobs, growing wages, upward mobility, innovation, progress, and higher standards of living.

In our annual ranking of the most competitive tax systems, we found for the 10th year in a row that Estonia has the best tax code in the OECD.[55] This is in part because it has a fully integrated income tax system that avoids double-taxing corporate income through taxes at both the entity and shareholder levels. Instead of a complicated corporate income tax and separate rules that apply to passthrough businesses, all businesses are subject to a simple 20 percent tax on distributed profits (including dividends and stock

50 Joint Committee on Taxation, "Revenue Estimates and Distributional Analyses," Aug. 3, 2021, https://www.finance.senate.gov/imo/media/doc/jct_analysis_on_corporate_tax_increase.pdf.
51 Cristina Enache, "Corporate Tax Rates around the World, 2022," Tax Foundation. December 13, 2022, https://taxfoundation.org/corporate-tax-rates-by-country-2022/.
52 OECD, Tax Database Table II.4. Overall Statutory Tax Rates on Dividend Income, https://www.oecd.org/tax/tax-policy/tax-database/; Elke Asen, "Double Taxation of Corporate Income in the United States and the OECD," Tax Foundation, January 13, 2021, https://taxfoundation.org/double-taxation-of-corporate-income/.
53 Scott Eastman, "Corporate and Pass-through Business Income and Returns Since 1980," Apr. 23, 2019, https://www.taxfoundation.org/pass-through-business-income-since-1980/
54 TaxEDU, "Principles of Sound Tax Policy," Tax Foundation, https://taxfoundation.org/principles/.
55 Alex Mengden, "International Tax Competitiveness Index, 2023," Tax Foundation, Oct. 18, 2023, https://taxfoundation.org/research/all/global/2023-international-tax-competitiveness-index/.

buybacks). At the individual level, a simple flat tax of 20 percent applies to all individual income except dividends, since they are already taxed by the distributed profits tax. Capital gains are taxed as ordinary income at 20 percent. Rather than a complicated estate tax like ours that taxes accumulated savings at death, bequeathed assets are simply taxed as capital gains when sold by the heir with deductible basis determined only by costs incurred by the heir.[56]

Simplicity and neutrality are the hallmarks of the Estonian income tax system.[57] Taxes are so simple in Estonia that they can typically be filed in five minutes, and the cost of compliance for businesses is among the lowest of any country.[58] Estonia's tax system is also very pro-growth, increasing small business entrepreneurship, investment, labor productivity and thereby wages.[59] Estonia's income tax system does all of this while generating substantial revenue comparable to other developed countries.[60]

We recently analyzed the effect of a revenue-neutral reform of the U.S. tax code along the lines of the Estonian income tax system, keeping only certain features of the current code that benefit low-income households (such as the EITC and Child Tax Credit) and support saving (such as 401ks).[61] By greatly simplifying the federal tax code, these reforms would substantially reduce compliance costs, potentially saving U.S. taxpayers more than $100 billion annually, comprised of more than $70 billion in reduced compliance costs for businesses and more than $30 billion in reduced compliance costs for individuals related to individual income and estate tax returns.

In addition to compliance cost savings, our modeling of the reform's impacts on the U.S. economy indicates it would increase GDP by 2.5 percent in the long run, grow the capital stock by 3.4 percent, add 1.3 million full-time equivalent jobs and raise wages by 1.4 percent. By increasing GDP, we estimate the reform would reduce the debt burden as measured by the debt-to-GDP ratio by 9.2 percentage points over the long run.

Distributionally, we find the reform would increase after-tax income overall by 3.5 percent in the long-run, accounting for improved economic growth, with a larger boost of 4.3 percent for the bottom quintile of earners and 4.7 percent for the second quintile.

56   William McBride, "Biden's New Tax Proposals are Complicated and Rife with Double Taxation," Tax Foundation, Mar. 13, 2023, https://taxfoundation.org/biden-tax-fairness/.

57   Estonia's simple approach to taxing business and individual income has also been implemented in Latvia and Georgia. Daniel Bunn, "Better than the Rest," Tax Foundation, Oct. 9, 2019, https://taxfoundation.org/estonia-tax-system-latvia-tax-system/; Gia Jandieri, "Tax Reform in Georgia 2004-2012," Tax Foundation, July 17, 2019, https://taxfoundation.org/tax-reforms-in-georgia-2004-2012/.

58   Kyle Pomerleau, "The Best Part of the Estonian Tax Code Is Not 5 Minute Tax Filing," Tax Foundation, Jul. 21, 2015, https://taxfoundation.org/best-part-estonian-tax-code-not-5-minute-tax-filing/; William McBride, Garrett Watson, Erica York, "Taxing Distributed Profits Makes Business Taxation Simple and Efficient," Tax Foundation, Mar. 1, 2023, https://taxfoundation.org/distributed-profits-tax-us-businesses/.

59   Jaan Maaso, Jaanika Merikull, and Priit Vahter, "Gross Profit Taxation Versus Distributed Profit Taxation and Firm Performance: Effects of Estonia's Corporate Income Tax Reform," The University of Tartu Faculty of Economics and Business Administration Working Paper No. 81-2011, March 23, 2011, https://ssrn.com/abstract=1793143 or http://dx.doi.org/10.2139/ssrn.1793143; Jaan Masso and Jaanika Merikull, "Macroeconomic Effects of Zero Corporate Income Tax on Retained Earnings," Baltic Journal of Economics, 11:2 (2011): 81-99, https://www.tandfonline.com/doi/pdf/10.1080/1406099X.2011.10840502; Aaro Hazak, "Companies' Financial Decisions Under the Distributed Profit Taxation Regime of Estonia," Emerging Markets Finance & Trade 45:4 (2009): 4-12, https://www.jstor.org/stable/27750676; Eduardo Davila and Benjamin Hebert, "Optimal Corporate Taxation under Financial Frictions," NBER Working Paper No. 25520, October 2021, https://www.nber.org/papers/w25520.

60   Over the last 10 years, Estonia's central government tax collections from income and profit amount to about 7.4 percent of GDP, compared to 7.3 percent for the median OECD country and 8.4 percent averaged across OECD countries. See OECD Tax Revenue Statistics, https://stats.oecd.org/index.aspx

61   William McBride, Huaqun Li, Garrett Watson, Alex Durante, Erica York, and Alex Muresianu, "Details and Analysis of a Tax Reform Plan for Growth and Opportunity," Tax Foundation, Jun. 29, 2023, https://taxfoundation.org/growth-opportunity-us-tax-reform-plan/

As top priority, lawmakers should simplify the tax code so that taxpayers can understand the laws and the IRS can administer them with minimum cost and frustration. As the IRS's National Taxpayer Advocate states in their most recent report to Congress, "Simplifying the Code is the most important step Congress can take to reduce taxpayer compliance burdens. Simplification is essential to the integrity of the U.S. tax system and will enhance voluntary compliance."[69] We have outlined reforms that would reduce taxpayer compliance burdens by at least $100 billion per year.

Second, lawmakers should reduce the economic drag caused by the tax code, particularly in the current environment of high interest rates and still-too-high inflation reducing living standards and prosperity. The tax code is one of the most effective levers available to lawmakers to strengthen the economy, but it should not be done through preferences that are targeted and complicated. Rather, lawmakers should broadly improve incentives to work, save, and invest by lowering marginal tax rates on individual and corporate income.

We have shown that revenue-neutral tax reform can greatly improve economic growth, increasing GDP by 2.5 percent in the long run, adding 1.3 million jobs, and raising wages by 1.4 percent such that after-tax incomes for the bottom 40 percent of earners increase by more than 4 percent on average. Additionally, the experience of other countries shows that taxing consumption as opposed to income raises substantial revenue in a more economically efficient way. To address distributional concerns, lawmakers can design consumption taxes to progressively tax the consumption of higher earners without the administrative complexity and compliance costs of our current progressive income tax system.

Contact

William McBride

Vice President of Federal Tax Policy and Stephen J. Entin Fellow in Economics
wmcbride@taxfoundation.org

The Tax Foundation is the nation's leading tax policy research organization. Since 1937, our research, analysis, and experts have informed smarter tax policy at the federal, state, and global levels. We are a 501(c)(3) nonprofit organization.

---

69   Internal Revenue Service National Taxpayer Advocate, "2022 Annual Report to Congress," Jan. 11, 2023, https://www.taxpayeradvocate.irs.gov/news/national-tax-payer-advocate-delivers-2022-annual-report-to-congress/.

More generally, the U.S. could learn from the experience of other countries in the OECD, which rely more heavily on consumption taxes than the U.S. does.[62] Value-added taxes (VATs) are a major source of revenue in virtually every developed country except the U.S., and as the literature cited above indicates, VATs and other taxes on consumption are among the least economically harmful ways to raise revenue.[63]

OECD countries have also tended to abandon more complicated means of taxing high earners such as wealth taxes due to their administrative and economic challenges.[64] Rather than high capital gains taxes, or any attempt to tax unrealized capital gains, most OECD countries have lower capital gains tax rates than the U.S., and tax capital income overall at lower average tax rates.[65]

Consumption taxes can be designed to progressively tax the consumption of higher earners without the administrative complexity and compliance costs of our current progressive income tax system. For example, by splitting the VAT base in two, businesses would pay taxes on their cash flow (sales less purchases and compensation paid), while households would pay taxes on compensation received. Applying a progressive rate schedule at the household level, with the top rate matching the rate on business cash flow, is a relatively simple way to achieve progressivity within a consumption tax.[66] Under a more standard value-added tax, the most efficient way to increase progressivity would be to offer targeted relief to lower- and middle-income households.[67]

We have recently modeled specific reforms that would shift the U.S tax system towards taxing consumption rather than income while simplifying the tax code's various anti-poverty programs, including an option that combines a cash flow tax with a progressive household compensation tax and per person credit. We find these reforms would lead to higher economic output and higher after-tax income for lower-income households while raising roughly the same amount of tax revenue for the federal government.[68]

Conclusion

We as a country have built a federal tax system that is inherently complex, costly, and controversial, one that is centered on taxing both individual and business income at progressive tax rates and littered with various preferences. To the extent it is comprehensible at all, taxpayers do not perceive it as fair. The IRS has real challenges administering such a complicated tax system, but boosting the IRS budget will not fix the underlying problem that causes taxpayers to call the IRS millions of times per year asking for help filling tax forms that take them more than 6.5 billion hours to complete.

62 Daniel Bunn and Cecilia Perez Weigel, "Sources of Government Revenue in the OECD," Tax Foundation, Feb. 23, 2023, https://taxfoundation.org/oecd-tax-revenue-by-country-2023/.

63 William McBride, "What Is the Evidence on Taxes and Growth," Tax Foundation, Dec. 18, 2012, https://www.taxfoundation.org/what-evidence-taxes-and-growth/.

64 Daniel Bunn, "What the U.S. Can Learn from the Adoption (and Repeal) of Wealth Taxes in the OECD," Tax Foundation, Jan. 18, 2022, https://taxfoundation.org/wealth-taxes-in-the-oecd/.

65 Daniel Bunn and Elke Asen, "Savings and Investment: The Tax Treatment of Stock and Retirement Accounts in the OECD," Tax Foundation, May 26, 2021, https://taxfoundation.org/savings-and-investment-oecd/#Capital; Jacob Lundberg and Johannes Nathell, "Taxing Capital—An International Comparison," Tax Foundation, May 11, 2021, https://taxfoundation.org/tax-burden-on-capital-income/.

66 This design is known as the "X Tax," developed by the late economist David Bradford. See Robert Carroll and Alan D. Viard, Progressive Consumption Taxation: The X Tax. (Washington, D.C: The Rowman & Littlefield Publishing Group, 2012).

67 See Rita de la Feria and Michael Walpole, "The Impact of Public Perceptions on General Consumption Taxes," British Tax Review 67.5 (Dec. 4, 2020), 637-669, https://papers.ssrn.com/sol3/papers.cfm?abstract_id=3723750 for a discussion on how other approaches, such as exemptions or reduced rates can, counterintuitively, increase regressivity by providing more benefits to higher-income households.

68 Erica York, Garrett Watson, Alex Durante, and Huaqun Li, "How Taxing Consumption Would Improve Long-Term Opportunity and Well-Being for Families and Children," Tax Foundation, Oct. 12, 2023, https://taxfoundation.org/research/all/federal/us-consumption-tax-vs-income-tax/.

About the Author

John graduated from the University of Illinois with a degree in accounting and shortly thereafter passed the CPA exam. His career in accounting, taxes and business spanned many years and many different aspects of accounting and taxes. He started with a national CPA firm and founded a local accounting firm which was then merged into a national firm. He worked for manufacturing companies and for half of his career for a community bank. In all these endeavors, he held various positions in income tax planning and compliance. He was responsible for the preparation of over 5000 income tax returns and learned all the complexities of compliance and planning in those positions.

Recently in retirement, John participated in a national income tax return training course and was astonished to see all the complexities that had been added to the tax law since his active involvement in that field. John told himself this couldn't be possible and set out to write "Tax Free at Last," a book he hopes will confirm his own opinion that the income tax law is unfair and unfathomable. The income tax law must be simplified and designed to help those with lower income and include a plan to restore the solvency of the Federal government. This book is a result of many years' experience in the field and many months of analysis of the sorry state of today's income tax law.

John divides his retirement time between Texas and Wisconsin. He and his wife Linda enjoy the company as much as possible of their five children and 11 grandchildren. He hopes this book will give them a better income tax law and a solvent Federal government.